As always, to my beloved family—
I love watching you feed your little ones' hearts and minds
with the Bread of Life.

May you all grow stronger in the Lord
with the passing years.

I love you more than the whole wide world!

CONTENTS

BISCUITS AND
SCONES

BREADS
(YEAST AND QUICK)

MUFFINS

ROLLS AND BUNS

RECIPE INDEX

THE AMISH AND THEIR COOKING TRADITIONS

I love writing about the Amish, and especially their cooking traditions. Not much that's fancy comes from Amish kitchens. Instead, the mouthwatering meals produced are meant to satisfy the hunger pangs of hardworking folks, and the ingredients often come from their land or from neighboring gardens and farms. Straightforward, uncomplicated, and trouble-free, the recipes you'll find in these pages have stood the test of time and are just the thing to round out a meal or to stand alone as the perfect snack. Also, the Amish keep busy most every day, so—with the exception of the yeast bread recipes—what you'll find here are quick-to-prepare baked goods that are big on taste…mouthwatering biscuits, hearty breads, tasty muffins, and delicious rolls and buns.

Because of this down-to-earth approach to mealtime, even beginner cooks can have success. Oh sure, there's always a learning curve when making something new, but even yeast bread isn't difficult—most of the process consists of allowing the dough to rise while you move on to something else. And the results? Just watch as your loved ones come home and catch their first whiff of fresh-from-the-oven dinner rolls, or dig into a loaf of quick bread for a midafternoon snack. To borrow from Proverbs 31:28, they'll rise up and call you blessed!

So pour yourself a cup of tea, settle into a comfy chair, and read through these recipes. I'm sure that very soon indeed you'll find a recipe that tempts you to hurry into the kitchen and start baking. And as you work to feed your family, take the time to thank God for your blessings. The more you practice thankfulness, the easier those thankful thoughts will come to you, and before you know it, you'll be living a joyful life, the result of which will be closer ties with your loved ones and a happy family.

My prayer for all women—young or old, single or married, childless or bursting at the seams with little ones—is that, like the Amish, you will find great joy in your home life and "lead a quiet and peaceable life in all godliness and honesty" (1 Timothy 2:2 kjv).

May God's richest blessings be yours!

Georgia

BISCUITS AND SCONES

Comfort food. That's what biscuits are to me. Slathered with butter and possibly a dollop of honey or jam, biscuits add that perfect touch to almost any meal. Even better? Biscuits are quick and easy to make, and the payoff in taste more than makes up for the little bit of effort and minimal ingredients required to make them.

I often make biscuits when I need something to add to a meal at the last minute. And when that's the case, I'll simply make the dough, add a splash or two of extra liquid so they are a bit on the soft side, and then drop the dough in rough mounds onto my baking sheet instead of going to the trouble to roll them out and cut them. It saves even more time, and even though they may not look as pretty as the rolled-out version, my drop biscuits taste just as good. Really, you can't go wrong when biscuits are on the menu.

I hope you find something new in this chapter besides the tried-and-true buttermilk biscuits (which, of course, are always a good choice). Give a few of these recipes a try and see if you don't find a new family favorite. I'm fairly certain you will.

Let them give thanks to the LORD
for his unfailing love
and his wonderful deeds for mankind,
for he satisfies the thirsty and fills
the hungry with good things.

PSALM 107:8-9

Lord, please bring to my mind often that Your
unfailing love for me satisfies me in ways that
nothing else can. My soul hungers for You. I want
to nourish my heart with Your Word. Help me to
practice thankfulness in all things, and learn to
trust Your path for me, even when the way is dark
and I can't see my destination. Even so, Lord, I
will praise Your name and give You thanks. Amen.

1 Angel Biscuits

4½ tsp. (2 packages) active dry yeast
¼ cup warm water (about 110°F)
2 cups warm buttermilk (about 110°F)
5 cups all-purpose flour
⅓ cup sugar
2 tsp. salt
2 tsp. baking powder
1 tsp. baking soda
1 cup shortening
melted butter for brushing tops of baked biscuits

In a small bowl, mix together the yeast and warm water. Let it stand for 5 minutes. Stir in the warm buttermilk. Set aside.

In a large bowl, mix together the flour, sugar, salt, baking powder, and baking soda. Cut in the shortening until the mixture resembles coarse cornmeal. Stir in the yeast mixture.

Turn the dough out onto a lightly floured surface and knead gently for about 30 seconds. Roll out the dough to ½-inch thickness and cut with a biscuit cutter. Place the biscuits on a lightly greased baking sheet with their sides not quite touching, cover, and let rise until double, about 30 to 45 minutes.

Bake in a preheated 450° oven 8 to 10 minutes or until done. Remove from the oven and immediately brush the tops with melted butter.

Notes:

2 Bacon and Cheese Drop Biscuits

2 cups all-purpose flour
4 tsp. baking powder
½ tsp. salt
5 T. shortening
⅓ cup Cheddar cheese
4 to 6 slices bacon, cooked and crumbled
1 cup milk

Preheat the oven to 450°.

In a large bowl, mix together the flour, baking powder, and salt. Cut in the shortening until the mixture resembles coarse crumbles. Mix in the cheese and bacon. Make a well in the center and pour in the milk all at once. Stir with a fork until the dough is mixed thoroughly and sticks mostly together in a soft ball.

Drop by heaping tablespoons onto a greased baking sheet and bake for 15 to 20 minutes or until done.

Notes:

3 Basic Biscuits

2 cups all-purpose flour
4 tsp. baking powder
½ tsp. salt
⅓ cup shortening
¾ cup milk

Preheat the oven to 450°.

In a large bowl, sift together the flour, baking powder, and salt. Cut in the shortening until the mixture resembles coarse cornmeal. Make a well in the center and pour the milk into the well all at once. Stir with a fork until the dough comes clean from the sides of the bowl.

Turn the dough out onto a lightly floured surface and knead it gently about 10 times. Roll or pat the dough to ½-inch thickness and cut the biscuits using a biscuit cutter or the top of a glass that has been dredged in flour to prevent the dough from sticking to the glass. Place biscuits on an ungreased baking sheet about 1 inch apart. Bake for 15 to 20 minutes or until done.

Notes:

4 Buttermilk Biscuits

2 cups all-purpose flour
½ tsp. salt
3 tsp. baking powder
½ tsp. baking soda
3 T. shortening
1 cup buttermilk

Preheat the oven to 425°.

Sift together the flour, salt, baking powder, and baking soda. Cut in the shortening until the mixture resembles coarse crumbles. Add the buttermilk all at once and mix with a fork until it forms a ball. Turn out the dough onto a floured surface and knead for 30 seconds. Roll out the dough to ½-inch thickness and then cut with a biscuit cutter.

Place the biscuits on an ungreased baking sheet and bake for 15 minutes or until golden brown and done.

Notes:

5 Cheesy Buttermilk Biscuits

2 cups all-purpose flour
¾ tsp. salt
3 tsp. baking powder
1 tsp. baking soda
¼ cup shortening
1 cup shredded Cheddar cheese
1 cup buttermilk

Preheat the oven to 425°.

In a large bowl, mix together the flour, salt, baking powder, and baking soda. Cut in the shortening until the mixture resembles coarse crumbles. Add the cheese and stir to mix thoroughly. Add the buttermilk all at once and mix with a fork until it forms a ball.

Turn out the dough onto a floured surface and knead for 30 seconds. Roll or pat the dough to ½-inch thickness and then cut with a biscuit cutter.

Place the biscuits on a greased baking sheet (or you can use a silicone baking sheet) and bake for 15 minutes or until done.

Notes:

6 Cheesy Garlic Biscuits

2 cups homemade biscuit mix or Bisquick
⅔ cup milk
⅔ cup Cheddar cheese
⅓ cup butter
¼ tsp. garlic powder, more or less to suit taste
¼ tsp. (heaping) dried parsley
a few shakes of salt from your salt shaker
one shake of pepper

Preheat the oven to 400°.

In a medium bowl, stir together the biscuit mix, milk, and Cheddar cheese; don't overmix.

Drop by large spoonfuls onto an ungreased cookie sheet, or a cookie sheet lined with a silicone baking mat. Bake for about 10 minutes, or until the biscuits are golden on top and baked completely.

In the meantime, in a small saucepan over low heat, melt the butter; add the garlic powder, parsley, salt, and pepper, and gently stir to mix. Remove the biscuits from the oven, and while they are still on the baking sheet, immediately brush the tops of the biscuits generously with the melted butter mixture.

Notes:

7 Cheesy Sausage Biscuits

2 cups all-purpose flour
4 tsp. baking powder
½ tsp. salt
5 T. shortening
⅓ cup Cheddar cheese
½ cup ground breakfast sausage, cooked, drained, and crumbled
1 cup milk

Preheat the oven to 450°.

In a large bowl, mix together the flour, baking powder, and salt. Cut in the shortening until the mixture resembles coarse crumbles. Mix in the cheese and sausage. Make a well in the center and pour in the milk all at once. Stir with a fork until the dough is mixed thoroughly and sticks mostly together in a soft ball.

Drop by heaping tablespoons onto a greased baking sheet and bake for 15 to 20 minutes or until done.

Notes:

8 Chopped Chicken Biscuits

2 cups all-purpose flour
4 tsp. baking powder
½ tsp. salt
3 T. shortening
¾ cup milk
2 cups cooked, chopped chicken (more or less—just use what
**   you have)**

Preheat the oven to 425°.

In a large bowl, mix together the flour, baking powder, and salt. Cut in the shortening until it resembles coarse crumbles. Add the milk all at once and mix well. Turn the dough out onto a floured work surface and knead about 25 times. Roll out the ball of dough to about ¼ inch thick. Cover generously with the chicken. Roll the dough up as you would a jelly roll and slice it into pieces that are about an inch thick. Place them on a greased cookie sheet about an inch apart.

Bake for 15 minutes.

Notes:

9 Cream Cheese Biscuits

2 cups all-purpose flour
1 T. baking powder
1 T. sugar
¾ tsp. salt
3 ounces very cold cream cheese, cut into small pieces
¼ cup shortening
½ cup green onions, finely chopped (I've used finely minced
**   yellow onions when I didn't have green onions)**
⅔ cup milk

Preheat the oven to 450°.

In a large bowl, combine the flour, baking powder, sugar, and salt. Cut in the cream cheese and shortening until the mixture resembles coarse crumbles. Stir in the green onions.

Make a well in the center of the flour mixture. Add the milk and stir with a fork to form a soft ball of dough. Turn out the dough onto a floured surface and knead for 30 seconds. Roll or pat the dough to ½-inch thickness and then cut with a biscuit cutter.

Place the biscuits on an ungreased baking sheet and bake for 10 to 12 minutes or until done.

Notes:

10 Cream Scones

2 cups all-purpose flour
3 tsp. baking powder
2 T. plus 2 tsp. sugar, divided
½ tsp. salt
¼ cup (½ stick) butter
2 eggs, one of them separated
⅓ cup whipping cream

Preheat the oven to 400°.

In a large mixing bowl, sift together the flour, baking powder, 2 tablespoons of the sugar, and the salt. Cut in the butter until the mixture resembles coarse crumbles.

In a separate bowl, separate the yolk of one of the eggs (reserve the egg white to brush the tops of the scones) and stir the yolk together with the other whole egg; then stir in the cream.

Make a well in the center of the flour mixture and pour the egg and cream mixture into the well; stir with a fork just until the dough pulls away from the sides of the bowl.

Sprinkle a clean surface with a small amount of flour. Using your hands, pat the dough into a ball and knead it on the floured surface for about 30 seconds. Divide the dough ball into 2 equal halves. Roll out each half into a 1-inch-thick circle (it will be about 6 inches in diameter). Cut each circle into 4 pie-shaped wedges and place them on an ungreased baking sheet about 1 inch apart. Brush the tops with the reserved egg white, and then sprinkle the tops with the remaining 2 teaspoons of sugar.

Notes:

Bake for 15 minutes or until done but not too dark. The scones are good plain, but they are even better when topped with jam and sweetened whipped cream.

11 Dried Sweet Cherry or Blueberry Biscuits

2 cups all-purpose flour
2 T. sugar
4 tsp. baking powder
½ tsp. salt
½ tsp. dried rosemary
½ cup (1 stick) very cold butter, cut into small pieces
¾ cup milk
½ cup dried cherries or blueberries, chopped

Preheat the oven to 425°.

In a large bowl, mix together the flour, sugar, baking powder, salt, and rosemary. Cut in the butter until the mixture resembles coarse crumbles. Make a well in the center and add the milk; stir to form a soft dough. Stir in the cherries (or blueberries).

Turn out the dough onto a floured surface and knead for 30 seconds. Roll or pat the dough to 1-inch thickness and then cut with a biscuit cutter. Place the biscuits about 1 inch apart on an ungreased baking sheet (or you can use a silicone baking mat) and bake for 15 minutes or until done.

Notes:

12 Easy Drop Biscuits

2 cups all-purpose flour
4 tsp. baking powder
½ tsp. salt
5 T. shortening
1 cup milk

Preheat the oven to 450°.

In a large bowl, mix together the flour, baking powder, and salt. Cut in the shortening until the mixture resembles coarse crumbles. Make a well in the center and pour in the milk all at once. Stir with a fork until the dough is mixed thoroughly and sticks mostly together in a soft ball.

Drop by heaping tablespoons onto a greased baking sheet and bake for 15 to 20 minutes or until done.

Notes:

13 Ham and Cheese Biscuits

2 cups all-purpose flour
2 tsp. baking powder
½ tsp. baking soda
½ cup (1 stick) very cold butter, cut into small pieces
⅔ cup buttermilk
½ cup shredded cheese (Swiss works well)
2 ounces ham, diced

Preheat the oven to 450°.

Grease a baking sheet or use a silicone baking mat.

In a large bowl, combine the flour, baking powder, and baking soda. Cut in the butter until the mixture resembles coarse crumbles. Add the buttermilk and then stir with a fork to form a soft, sticky dough. Stir in the cheese and ham.

Turn out the dough onto a floured surface and knead for about 30 seconds. Roll or pat the dough to ½-inch thickness and then cut with a biscuit cutter. Place biscuits 2 inches apart on the prepared baking sheet.

Bake for about 10 minutes or until the biscuits are golden brown and done.

Notes:

14 Herbed Biscuits

2 cups all-purpose flour
2 tsp. baking powder
¼ tsp. baking soda
1 tsp. salt
¼ tsp. dry mustard
½ tsp. sage
½ tsp. celery seed
¼ cup shortening
¾ cup buttermilk

Preheat the oven to 425°.

In a large bowl, mix together the dry ingredients and herbs. Cut in the shortening until the mixture resembles coarse crumbles. Add the buttermilk and stir using a fork until a soft dough forms.

Turn out the dough onto a floured surface and knead about 20 times. Roll or pat the dough to ½-inch thickness and then cut with a biscuit cutter.

Place the biscuits on an ungreased baking sheet and bake for about 10 minutes or until done.

Notes:

15 Lard Biscuits

2 cups all-purpose flour
4 tsp. baking powder
½ tsp. salt
3 T. lard
¾ cup milk

Preheat the oven to 450°.

In a large bowl, mix together the flour, baking powder, and salt. Using a fork, cut in the lard until the mixture resembles coarse crumbles. Make a well in the center and pour the milk into the well all at once. Mix with the fork until a soft dough forms. Then use one of your hands to gently knead the dough right in the bowl, about 10 to 15 times.

Turn the dough out onto a lightly floured surface and roll or pat to ½-inch thickness. Cut with a biscuit or cookie cutter and place the biscuits on a greased baking sheet.

Bake for 12 minutes or until the biscuits are a light golden brown and done.

Notes:

16 Light-as-Air Biscuits

2 cups all-purpose flour
½ tsp. salt
2 tsp. sugar
4 tsp. baking powder
½ tsp. cream of tartar
½ cup shortening
⅔ cup milk

Preheat the oven to 450°.

In a large bowl, mix together the flour, salt, sugar, baking powder, and cream of tartar. Cut in the shortening until the mixture resembles coarse crumbles. Make a well in the center and add the milk all at once; stir with a fork until the dough leaves the sides of the bowl.

Turn out the dough onto a lightly floured surface and knead about 5 times. Roll or pat the dough to ½-inch thickness and then cut with a biscuit cutter.

Place the biscuits on an ungreased baking sheet and bake for 15 minutes or until done.

Notes:

17 Maple Nut Scones

3½ cups all-purpose flour
1 cup nuts, finely chopped (walnuts or pecans are good in this
    recipe)
4 tsp. baking powder
1 tsp. salt
⅔ cup chilled butter, cut into small pieces
1 cup milk
½ cup maple syrup
sugar for sprinkling (coarse sugar if you have it, but regular
    granulated will work also)

Preheat the oven to 425°.

In a large bowl, whisk together the flour, nuts, baking powder, and salt. Cut in the chilled butter until the mixture resembles coarse crumbles. Add the milk and maple syrup and stir to mix; the dough should hold together but be soft. Turn out onto a very lightly floured surface and knead about 5 to 8 times. Roll out the dough into a circle about ½ inch thick. Cut into 10 to 12 wedges and place on a greased baking sheet. Sprinkle the tops with a bit of sugar.

Bake for 15 to 18 minutes or until done.

Notes:

18 Orange Cream Scones

2 cups all-purpose flour
3 tsp. baking powder
2 T. plus 2 tsp. sugar, divided
½ tsp. salt
¼ cup (½ stick) butter
2 eggs, one of them separated
⅓ cup whipping cream
3 tsp. grated orange peel
¼ tsp. vanilla

Preheat the oven to 400°.

In a large mixing bowl, sift together the flour, baking powder, 2 tablespoons of the sugar, and salt. Cut in the butter until the mixture resembles coarse crumbles.

In a separate bowl, separate the yolk of one of the eggs (reserve the egg white to brush the tops of the scones), and stir the yolk together with the other whole egg. Then stir in the cream, orange peel, and vanilla.

Make a well in the center of the flour mixture, and pour the egg and cream mixture into the well; stir with a fork just until the dough pulls away from the sides of the bowl.

Sprinkle a clean surface with a small amount of flour. Using your hands, pat the dough into a ball and knead it on the floured surface for about 30 seconds. Divide the dough ball into 2 equal halves. Roll out each half into a 1-inch-thick circle (it will be about 6 inches in diameter). Cut each circle into 4 pie-shaped wedges and place them on an ungreased baking sheet about 1 inch apart. Brush the tops with the reserved egg white, and then sprinkle the tops with the remaining 2 teaspoons of sugar.

Notes:

Bake for 15 minutes or until done but not too dark. The scones are good plain, but they are even better when topped with jam and sweetened whipped cream.

19 Pumpkin Biscuits

2½ cups all-purpose flour
¼ cup brown sugar
1 T. baking powder
¾ tsp. salt
¾ tsp. ground cinnamon
¼ tsp. ground ginger
¼ tsp. ground allspice
½ cup shortening
½ cup chopped nuts (walnuts or pecans are good choices)
¾ cup canned pumpkin
½ cup milk

Preheat the oven to 450°.

In a large bowl, mix together the flour, brown sugar, baking powder, salt, cinnamon, ginger, and allspice. Cut in the shortening until the mixture resembles coarse crumbles. Stir in the nuts.

In a small bowl, beat together the pumpkin and milk until smooth. Add to the flour mixture and stir with a fork to form a soft dough.

Turn out the dough onto a floured surface and knead for 30 seconds. Roll or pat the dough to ½-inch thickness and then cut with a biscuit cutter. Place the biscuits on a greased baking sheet and bake for 12 to 14 minutes or until done and a light golden brown.

Notes:

20 Savory Potato and Vegetable Scones

2½ to 3 cups all-purpose flour
1 T. plus 1 tsp. baking powder
1½ tsp. salt
⅛ tsp. dried sage
⅛ tsp. dried rosemary
4 ounces cream cheese
½ cup shredded Cheddar cheese
1 egg
1 cup cream
¼ cup finely diced green, red, yellow, and/or orange bell peppers
(using multiple colors isn't necessary, but it makes the
scones prettier)
¼ cup finely diced onions
½ large potato, peeled, cooked, and finely diced
⅛ cup fresh, thinly sliced or diced mushrooms
1 T. butter

Preheat the oven to 400°.

In a medium bowl, mix together dry ingredients and set aside.

In a large bowl, cream together the cream cheese, shredded Cheddar, and egg. Add the cream and mix well.

On medium-low heat, sauté the vegetables in butter until soft, about 4 minutes. Add them to the cream mixture and stir well. Add the dry ingredients and stir by hand until a soft dough forms.

Pat out the dough into a 1-inch-thick circle. Place the circle on a buttered cookie sheet (or you can use a silicone baking mat instead) and

Notes:

then, using a pizza cutter or knife, cut it into 8 equal wedges (as if you were cutting pie).

Bake for 20 to 25 minutes or until done. Remove the scones from the baking sheet and set on a wire rack to cool.

21 Sour Cream Biscuits

⅔ cup milk
⅔ cup sour cream
2 cups all-purpose flour
1 T. sugar
3 tsp. baking powder
½ tsp. salt
¼ cup shortening

Preheat the oven to 450°.

In a medium bowl, mix together the milk and sour cream until well blended; set aside.

In a large bowl, mix together the flour, sugar, baking powder, and salt. Cut the shortening into the flour mixture until it resembles coarse crumbles. Make a well in the center and pour in the sour cream mixture all at once; stir just until blended.

Drop by large tablespoonfuls onto a greased baking sheet and bake for 10 to 12 minutes or until done.

Notes:

22 Yogurt and Sour Cream Biscuits

BISCUITS AND SCONES

2 cups all-purpose flour
1 T. sugar
2 tsp. baking powder
½ tsp. baking soda
½ tsp. salt
¼ tsp. oregano
¼ cup (½ stick) very cold butter, cut into small pieces
⅔ cup plain yogurt
½ cup milk
¼ cup sour cream
½ cup finely chopped green onions or chives

Preheat the oven to 400°.

Line a baking sheet with parchment paper or a silicone baking mat, or generously grease the baking sheet.

In a large bowl, combine the flour, sugar, baking powder, baking soda, salt, and oregano. Cut in the butter until the mixture resembles coarse crumbles. Add the yogurt, milk, and sour cream and stir gently to form a soft, sticky dough. Stir in the green onions. Using about ¼ cup for each biscuit, drop the dough 2 inches apart onto the prepared baking sheet.

Bake for 15 minutes or until the biscuits are a light golden brown.

Notes:

BREADS
(YEAST AND QUICK)

Baking bread is as much an art as it is a step-by-step procedure. When you are just starting out, following a recipe will give you a sense of confidence. But hopefully there will come a time when you decide to quit with the careful measuring and mix together your loaves by feel. This is when your bread-baking skills will really shine and you'll develop your own signature-style loaves.

Yeast breads are best made when you have several hours to devote to the process, but quick breads can be made in very little time and are a great choice for a last-minute addition to a meal or when unexpected guests show up. Both types of bread have their place in the family kitchen.

If you choose to use organic ingredients and grind your wheat and other grains, you can save a fair amount of money over store-bought loaves. Buying in bulk will increase this savings. And because most quick breads don't seem to have a store-bought equivalent, your loved ones will enjoy the special treat. If you are new to bread baking, without a doubt the easiest recipe in this section is the Buttermilk Whole Wheat Quick Bread—with only 5 ingredients. You'll be surprised how effortless it will be to produce an exceptionally tasty treat. And if you have several hours to devote to your baking, you can't go wrong with fresh yeast bread, such as Honey Whole Wheat Bread, Egg Bread (it's great for sandwiches!), or German Dark Rye Bread.

May grain abound throughout the land;
on the tops of the hills may it sway.
May the crops flourish like Lebanon
and thrive like the grass of the field.

PSALM 72:16

Heavenly Father, thank You for the gift of this
day. Please bless the work of my hands as I tend
to the needs of my family, and help me find ways
to draw them closer to You—for Your ways are
perfect, and You are the true head of this household.
May Your Spirit dwell richly in all of us. Amen.

23 Apple Bread

½ cup (1 stick) butter, room temperature
1 cup sugar
2 eggs
1 tsp. vanilla
2 cups all-purpose flour
1 T. baking soda
½ tsp. salt
⅓ cup sour milk (or ⅓ cup sour cream)
1 cup chopped apples
⅓ cup chopped walnuts

Preheat the oven to 350°.

In a large bowl, cream together the butter and sugar. Add the eggs and vanilla and beat well.

In another bowl, mix together the flour, baking soda, and salt. Add the dry ingredients alternately with the milk to the butter mixture; blend well after each addition. Stir in the apples and walnuts.

Pour the batter in a greased loaf pan and bake for 55 minutes or until done.

Notes:

24 Applesauce Nut Bread

1½ cups all-purpose flour
1 tsp. baking powder
1 tsp. baking soda
1 tsp. salt
1 tsp. cinnamon
½ tsp. nutmeg
1 cup rolled oats
½ cup chopped walnuts
½ cup raisins
⅓ cup shortening
½ cup brown sugar
2 eggs
1 cup unsweetened applesauce
½ cup milk

Preheat the oven to 350°.

In a large mixing bowl, sift together the flour, baking powder, baking soda, salt, cinnamon, and nutmeg. Stir in the rolled oats, walnuts, and raisins.

In another bowl, cream together the shortening and brown sugar. Add the eggs and beat until light and fluffy. Blend in the applesauce and milk.

Add the creamed mixture to the dry ingredients and beat for 30 seconds. Although the batter will be lumpy, don't overbeat it. Pour the batter into a large, greased loaf pan and bake for 50 to 60 minutes.

Notes:

25 Banana Nut Bread

⅔ cup sugar
⅓ cup shortening
2 eggs
3 T. sour milk or buttermilk
1 cup mashed bananas (slightly overripe bananas work best)
2 cups all-purpose flour
1 tsp. baking powder
½ tsp. baking soda
½ tsp. salt
½ cup chopped walnuts

Preheat the oven to 350°.

Mix together the sugar, shortening, and eggs. (An electric mixer works best.) Stir in the sour milk and mashed bananas.

In another bowl, mix together the flour, baking powder, baking soda, and salt and blend into the banana mixture. Add the walnuts and stir to blend.

Pour the batter into a well-greased loaf pan. Let stand for 20 minutes; then bake for 50 to 60 minutes.

Notes:

26 Basic Per Loaf Bread

For each loaf you wish to make, use the following measurements.

1 cup warm water, about 110° (or use half water and half milk)
1 tsp. melted shortening, butter, or vegetable oil
1 scant tsp. salt
1 T. honey, sugar, or other sweetener
1 tsp. active dry yeast (for 4 loaves, use 1 rounded tablespoon)
3 cups all-purpose flour

In a mixing bowl, stir together the water, melted shortening, salt, and sugar. Sprinkle the yeast over the top of the mixture and let it stand until the yeast dissolves and starts bubbling a bit, about 10 minutes.

Stir in half of the flour (1½ cups flour for each loaf) and beat until smooth. You can use an electric mixer for this part if desired, but you can also mix by hand using a large wooden spoon. Add enough of the remaining flour to make a dough ball that holds together and comes away from the sides of the bowl.

Place the dough onto a floured work surface and knead well for 5 to 10 minutes, adding more flour as needed to keep the dough from sticking.

Put the dough into a large greased bowl and grease all the surfaces of the dough as well. Cover it with a towel and let it rise until double, about 1 to 1½ hours. Punch down and then lightly knead the dough for a minute or so, grease all the surfaces once again, and let it rise in the greased bowl a second time until double. Punch down the dough and form into a loaf (or however many loaves you've decided to make). Place the loaf seam side down into a greased loaf pan and let it rise until almost double, about 45 minutes.

Notes:

Preheat the oven to 400°. Place the loaf in the preheated oven and then immediately turn the heat down to 350°. Bake about 30 minutes or until done. Remove the loaf from the oven, grease the top if desired, take it out of the baking pan, and cool on a wire rack.

27 Black Bread

1⅓ cups strong brewed coffee (cooled to about 110°)
3 T. brown sugar
2½ tsp. active dry yeast
¼ cup cooking oil
¼ cup molasses
1 cup whole wheat flour
1 cup rye flour
2 T. unsweetened cocoa powder
1½ tsp. salt
2 cups all-purpose flour, more or less

In a medium bowl, mix together the coffee and brown sugar. Sprinkle the yeast on top of the mixture and let it stand until bubbly, about 10 minutes. Add the cooking oil and molasses.

In a large bowl, mix together the whole wheat flour, rye flour, cocoa powder, and salt. Add the yeast mixture and beat on medium (or beat by hand) for about 3 minutes. Gradually add the all-purpose flour, stirring to incorporate. When the dough ball begins to pull away from the sides of the bowl, turn out onto a floured work surface and knead for about 8 minutes, adding more flour as needed to keep the dough from sticking.

Notes:

Put the dough into a large greased bowl and grease all the surfaces of the dough as well. Cover the dough with a towel and let it rise until double, about 1½ to 2 hours. Punch down and then lightly knead the dough for a minute or so, grease all the surfaces once again, and let it rise in the greased bowl a second time until double, about 1 hour. Punch down the dough and form into 12 round rolls. Place the rolls onto a greased baking sheet, cover with a towel, and let them rise until almost double.

Bake in a preheated 375° oven for 20 to 25 minutes or until done.

28 Breadsticks

2¼ tsp. (1 package) active dry yeast
⅔ cup warm water (110° to 120°)
2 to 2½ cups all-purpose flour
1½ tsp. sugar
1 tsp. garlic salt (optional)
¼ cup shortening
1 T. water
1 egg white
sesame or poppy seeds for sprinkling on top

In a large bowl, dissolve the yeast in the warm water and allow to stand for about 5 minutes. Add 1 cup of the flour, sugar, garlic salt (if using), and shortening and beat with an electric mixer or large wooden spoon for about 3 minutes. Stir in the remainder of the flour and continue mixing until the dough forms a ball and begins to pull away from the sides of the bowl.

Notes:

Place the dough into a greased bowl, cover, and let it rise until doubled (about 40 to 45 minutes).

Turn out the dough onto a floured surface and knead for about one minute (the floured surface will help the dough lose its stickiness). Roll out the dough to a 15 x 10-inch rectangle and place it in a greased jelly roll pan of the same size. Cut the dough the short way into 12 even strips and then cut those strips in half for a total of 24 breadsticks. Combine 1 tablespoon water with the egg white and blend well. Brush the egg mixture onto the tops of the breadsticks, and then sprinkle with sesame or poppy seeds.

Cover and let rise for about 20 minutes. Meanwhile, preheat the oven to 375°.

Bake the breadsticks for 18 to 22 minutes or until golden brown.

---

29 Bubble Bread

1 cup milk, scalded and cooled to about 110°
½ cup plus 1 cup sugar, divided
1 tsp. salt
4½ tsp. (2 packages) active dry yeast
2 eggs, beaten
4½ cups all-purpose flour
1 T. cinnamon
½ cup (1 stick) butter

Mix together the milk, ½ cup of the sugar, and the salt. Add the yeast, eggs, and most of the flour. Turn out the dough onto a floured surface and knead for 8 minutes, adding flour as needed so the dough

Notes:

doesn't stick. Place the dough in a greased bowl, turning the dough so the entire surface is greased; cover and let it rise until doubled, about 1 to 1½ hours. Punch it down and let it rise until doubled again. Punch the dough down and let it rest for 10 minutes.

Meanwhile, in a small bowl, mix together the remaining 1 cup of sugar and the cinnamon. Melt the butter and place it in another small bowl.

Roll the dough into balls the size of a walnut; roll each ball in the melted butter and then the cinnamon sugar mixture, and place the balls in a greased angel food cake pan in staggered rows. Cover and let rise for 1 hour.

Preheat the oven to 350° and then bake the bread for 22 to 26 minutes or until done. Cool the bread for 10 minutes and then remove from the pan to a wire rack. Serve warm.

30 Buttermilk and Honey Bread

1 cup warm water (110°)
pinch of sugar
1½ T. active dry yeast
2 cups buttermilk
½ cup (1 stick) butter, melted, or vegetable oil
¼ cup honey
1 T. salt
7 to 7½ cups all-purpose flour

In a small bowl, combine ½ cup of the warm water with a pinch of sugar. Sprinkle the yeast over the liquid and let it stand until bubbly, about 10 minutes.

Notes:

42

In a large bowl, combine the remaining ½ cup warm water, buttermilk, melted butter, honey, and salt. Add the yeast mixture and stir until combined. Add 2 cups of the flour and mix well. Using an electric mixer or hand beaters, beat for about 3 minutes. Gradually add most of the remaining flour, stirring well after each addition, until the dough pulls away from the sides of the bowl.

Turn out the dough onto a floured work surface and knead, adding flour as necessary to prevent sticking, for 8 minutes.

Grease a large bowl and put the dough into the bowl, turning the dough so the entire surface is greased. Cover with a towel and let the dough rise until doubled, about 1 to 1½ hours.

Divide the dough in half and form into 2 loaves. Place in greased loaf pans, cover, and let rise until almost doubled, about 30 minutes. Meanwhile, preheat the oven to 350°.

Bake the bread for 40 to 45 minutes or until done. Remove the bread from the pans and allow it to cool on wire racks.

31 Buttermilk Whole Wheat Quick Bread

1 quart buttermilk
4 cups whole wheat flour
3 cups brown sugar
Pinch of salt
1 tsp. baking soda

Preheat the oven to 350°.

Mix together all ingredients and pour the batter into 2 greased loaf pans. Bake for 60 to 70 minutes.

Notes:

32 Carrot Nut Bread

BREADS
(YEAST AND QUICK)

1½ cups all-purpose flour
1 cup whole wheat flour
¾ cup brown sugar
1 tsp. baking soda
2½ tsp. baking powder
1 tsp. salt
2 T. shortening, melted
1 cup warm milk
2 eggs
1 cup grated peeled carrots
½ cup nuts, chopped

Preheat the oven to 375°.

In a medium bowl, whisk together the all-purpose flour, whole wheat flour, brown sugar, baking soda, baking powder, and salt; set aside.

In a large bowl, mix together the melted shortening, milk, and eggs. Add the flour mixture to the liquid mixture and stir to mix. Fold in the carrots and nuts.

Bake in a greased loaf pan for 50 to 60 minutes or until done. Allow to cool before slicing.

Notes:

33 Chocolate Zucchini Bread

3 eggs, beaten
1 cup cooking oil
1¾ cups sugar
1 T. vanilla
2 cups grated zucchini
3 cups all-purpose flour (or use half whole wheat and half all-purpose)
1 tsp. salt
1 tsp. baking soda
1 tsp. baking powder
½ cup unsweetened cocoa
½ cup chopped walnuts or pecans (optional)

BREADS (YEAST AND QUICK)

Preheat the oven to 350°.

In a large bowl, mix together the eggs, oil, sugar, and vanilla. Add the zucchini and stir.

In a separate bowl, mix together the flour, salt, baking soda, baking powder, and cocoa. Add the flour mixture to the zucchini mixture and blend well. Add the nuts, if using, and stir again.

Grease and flour 2 loaf pans. Pour in the batter.

Bake for 45 minutes. Cool the bread in the pans for 10 to 15 minutes. Remove the loaves to a wire rack to finish cooling.

Notes:

34 Corn Bread

¾ cup cornmeal
1 cup all-purpose flour
2 T. sugar
1 tsp. salt
3½ tsp. baking powder
1 cup milk
2 eggs
2 T. melted shortening or butter

Preheat the oven to 425°.

In a large bowl, mix together the cornmeal and flour. Add the sugar, salt, and baking powder and stir to mix. Next, add the milk, eggs, and melted shortening and mix together thoroughly. (You can use an electric mixer if you desire.)

Pour into a well-greased baking pan (9 x 9 inches or 8 x 10 inches) or a well-seasoned or greased cast-iron skillet. Bake for 25 minutes or until done.

Notes:

35 Corn Bread with Cheese and Bacon

1 cup all-purpose flour
1 cup cornmeal
½ cup instant dry milk
2 T. sugar
4 tsp. baking powder
½ tsp. salt
½ cup shredded Cheddar cheese
½ cup cooked, crumbled bacon (or you can use real bacon bits)
1 egg
1 cup water
¼ cup cooking oil

Preheat the oven to 425°.

In a large mixing bowl, combine the flour, cornmeal, instant milk, sugar, baking powder, and salt and stir to mix well. Add the cheese and bacon and stir well again.

In a medium bowl, beat the egg and then add the water and cooking oil, mixing until well blended. Stir into the cornmeal mixture. Beat by hand using a large wooden spoon just until well blended and smooth. Pour the batter into a greased loaf pan and bake for 20 to 25 minutes or until done and a light golden color.

Notes:

36 Corn Bread with Instant Milk Powder

1 cup all-purpose flour
1 cup cornmeal
½ cup instant dry milk
2 T. sugar
4 tsp. baking powder
½ tsp. salt
1 egg
1 cup water
¼ cup cooking oil

Preheat the oven to 425°.

In a mixing bowl, combine the flour, cornmeal, instant milk powder, sugar, baking powder, and salt and stir to mix well.

In a medium bowl, beat egg and then add water and cooking oil, beating until well blended. Stir into the cornmeal mixture. Beat by hand using a wooden spoon just until well blended and smooth. Pour batter into a greased loaf pan.

Bake for 20 minutes or until done and a light golden color.

Notes:

37 Corn Bread with Sour Cream

¾ cup cornmeal
1 cup all-purpose flour
1 tsp. baking soda
1 tsp. cream of tartar
1 tsp. salt
2½ T. sugar
1 egg, well beaten
2 T. (¼ stick) butter, melted
1 cup sour cream
¼ cup milk

Preheat the oven to 425°.

In a large bowl, whisk together the cornmeal and flour. Add the baking soda, cream of tartar, salt, and sugar and whisk again to mix together. Add the egg, melted butter, sour cream, and milk and beat until well mixed.

Pour the batter into a well-greased 9 x 9-inch baking pan and bake for 20 minutes or until done.

BREADS
(YEAST AND QUICK)

Notes:

38 Date Nut Bread

¾ cup brown sugar
½ cup (1 stick) butter, softened
2 eggs
2 cups all-purpose flour
1 tsp. baking powder
½ tsp. baking soda
½ tsp. salt
1 cup buttermilk
1 cup chopped dates
½ cup chopped walnuts
2 tsp. grated orange peel (optional)

BREADS
(YEAST AND QUICK)

Preheat the oven to 350°.

Grease and flour the bottom only of a loaf pan; set aside.

In a large bowl, beat together the sugar and butter until light and fluffy; beat in the eggs until well blended.

In another bowl, mix together the flour, baking powder, baking soda, and salt.

Add the flour mixture alternately with the buttermilk to the large bowl, mixing well after each addition. Stir in the dates, nuts, and orange peel (if using). Pour the batter into the prepared pan.

Bake for 55 to 60 minutes or until done. Cool for about 10 minutes; then remove the bread from the loaf pan and continue to cool on a wire rack.

Notes:

39 Egg Bread

1½ cups milk, scalded
½ cup (1 stick) butter
½ cup sugar plus ½ tsp. sugar, divided
½ cup warm water (110°)
4½ tsp. (2 packages) active dry yeast
2 eggs, beaten
9 cups all-purpose flour, more or less
2 tsp. salt

In a large mixing bowl, pour the scalded milk over the butter and ½ cup sugar; cool.

In a small bowl, stir the ½ tsp. sugar into the warm water and then stir in the yeast. Let it stand for 5 minutes.

Add the yeast mixture to the milk mixture and stir. Alternately add the eggs and 3 cups of the flour; then add the salt and beat for 3 minutes. By hand, continue adding the rest of the flour, and knead the dough for 8 to 10 minutes. Place the dough in a greased bowl, turning the dough so the entire surface is greased. Cover and let rise until double, about 1 to 1½ hours.

Shape the dough into 3 loaves and place it in greased loaf pans. Let it rise again until the dough is about one inch above the top of the loaf pans.

Bake at 425° for 10 minutes; then reduce the temperature to 350° and bake an additional 30 to 40 minutes.

Notes:

40 German Dark Rye Bread

3 cups all-purpose flour
4½ tsp. (2 packages) active dry yeast
¼ cup unsweetened cocoa powder
1 T. caraway seeds
2 cups water
⅓ cup molasses
2 T. (¼ stick) butter
1 T. sugar
1 T. salt
3 to 3½ cups rye flour
cooking oil, for brushing tops of loaves

In a large mixing bowl, combine the all-purpose flour, yeast, cocoa powder, and caraway seeds until well blended.

In a saucepan combine the water, molasses, butter, sugar, and salt; heat until just warm, stirring occasionally to mostly melt the butter. The temperature shouldn't be above 120°. Add to the dry mixture and beat at low speed for 30 seconds; then turn to medium speed and beat for 3 minutes more.

By hand, stir in enough rye flour to make a soft dough. Turn out onto a floured surface and knead until smooth, adding more rye flour as needed, about 5 minutes. Cover; let stand for 30 minutes.

Punch down and divide the dough in half. Shape each half into a round loaf; place on greased baking sheets or 2 greased pie plates. Brush the tops of the loaves with a little cooking oil. Slash the tops of the loaves with a sharp knife. Cover and let rise until doubled, about 1 to 1½ hours.

Bake in a preheated 400° oven for 25 to 35 minutes or until the bread looks done. Remove from the baking pans and cool on wire racks.

Notes:

41 Good for You Bread

3½ to 4 cups all-purpose flour
1¾ cups rye flour
1¾ cups whole wheat flour
2 tsp. salt
6¾ tsp. (3 packages) active dry yeast
1¾ cups milk
¾ cup water
⅔ cup honey
3 T. butter
2 T. molasses
½ cup shelled sunflower seeds
¼ cup wheat germ
¼ cup whole bran cereal

In a large bowl, mix together 2 cups of the all-purpose flour, the rye flour, and the whole wheat flour.

In another large bowl, mix together 3 cups of the flour mixture, salt, and yeast.

In a small saucepan, heat together the milk, water, honey, butter, and molasses to 120° to 130°. Add the warmed milk mixture to the 3 cups of flour mixture. With an electric mixer or a large wooden spoon, beat for about 3 minutes. Stir in the sunflower seeds, wheat germ, bran cereal, the remaining flour mixture, and most of the remaining all-purpose flour, until the dough begins to form a ball and leaves the sides of the bowl.

Turn out the dough onto a floured surface and knead for about 10 minutes, adding more of the all-purpose flour as needed. Place the

Notes:

dough in a greased bowl, turning the dough so the entire surface is greased, and cover with a towel. Let it rise in a warm place until doubled in size, about 1 to 1½ hours.

Punch down the dough, divide in half, shape each half into a ball, and allow to rest on the counter, covered, for 15 minutes.

Shape the dough balls into 2 loaves and place in 2 greased loaf pans. Cover and let rise until the dough is almost doubled, about 30 to 45 minutes.

Preheat the oven to 350° and bake for 40 to 45 minutes or until done. Remove the bread from the loaf pans and cool on a wire rack.

42 Herb Bubble Bread

1 cup milk, scalded and cooled to about 110°
1 T. sugar
1 tsp. salt
4½ tsp. (2 packages) active dry yeast
2 eggs, beaten
4½ cups all-purpose flour
½ cup Parmesan cheese
¾ tsp. dried parsley flakes
¼ tsp. dill weed
⅛ tsp. each dried thyme, basil, and rosemary
½ cup (1 stick) butter, melted
2 tsp. minced garlic

Mix together the milk, sugar, and salt. Add the yeast, eggs, and most of the flour. Turn out the dough onto a floured surface and knead for 8 minutes, adding more flour as needed so the dough doesn't stick.

Notes:

Place the dough in a greased bowl, turning the dough so the entire surface is greased; cover and let rise until doubled, about 1 to 1½ hours. Punch the dough down and let it rise until doubled again. Punch down and let it rest for 10 minutes.

Meanwhile, in a small bowl, mix together the Parmesan cheese, parsley flakes, dill weed, thyme, basil, and rosemary. In another small bowl, mix together the melted butter and minced garlic.

Roll the dough into balls the size of a walnut; roll them in the melted garlic butter and then the herb mixture and place them in a greased angel food cake pan in staggered rows. Cover and let rise for 1 hour.

Bake in a preheated 350° oven for 22 to 26 minutes or until done. Cool the bread for 10 minutes; then remove from the pan to a wire rack. Serve warm.

Notes:

43 Honey Corn Bread

1 cup cornmeal
1 cup all-purpose flour
1 T. baking powder
½ tsp. salt
1 cup buttermilk*
1 egg
¼ cup (½ stick) butter, melted
½ cup honey

Preheat the oven to 425°.

In a large bowl, mix together the cornmeal, flour, baking powder, and salt.

In a medium bowl, whisk together the buttermilk, egg, and melted butter until well blended. Add the honey and whisk again to mix well. Add the buttermilk mixture to the cornmeal mixture and mix by hand; don't overmix. (Batter will be lumpy.)

Grease or butter an 8 x 8-inch or 9 x 9-inch baking dish and pour the batter into the prepared pan. Bake for 20 to 25 minutes or until done.

---

* If you don't have any buttermilk on hand, you can use the same amount of regular milk. Just add a teaspoon of lemon juice or white vinegar and let it stand for about 5 minutes until it curdles slightly before adding to the other ingredients.

Notes:

44 Honey Whole Wheat Bread

4½ tsp. (2 packages) active dry yeast
2 cups warm water (110° to 120°)
2 cups warm milk (110° to 120°)
½ cup (1 stick) butter, softened, or ½ cup cooking oil
½ cup honey
¼ cup molasses
2 tsp. salt
9 to 10 cups whole wheat flour, more or less

In a small bowl, dissolve the yeast in warm water. Let it stand until bubbly, about 5 to 10 minutes.

In a large bowl, mix together the warm milk, butter, honey, molasses, and salt. Add the yeast mixture and stir to mix. Gradually add the flour, stirring with a wooden spoon until the dough comes away from the sides of the bowl and a soft dough forms. Turn out onto a floured surface and knead until smooth, about 8 to 10 minutes, adding small amounts of flour as needed.

Place the dough ball in a large greased or buttered bowl; cover and let rise until double, about 1½ to 2 hours. Punch down the dough and let it rest for several minutes; knead the dough about 20 times and then divide into 4 equal pieces. Shape each piece of dough into a loaf and place in greased loaf pans. Cover the dough and let it rise for about an hour or until almost doubled.

Bake in a preheated oven at 375° for 35 to 40 minutes or until done. Cool in the loaf pans for about 5 minutes and then turn out the loaves on a wire rack to finish cooling.

Note: This recipe makes 4 loaves. You can freeze what you won't eat right away; just make sure the bread is completely cool before wrapping tightly and freezing.

Notes:

45 Lemon Tea Bread

Bread
⅓ cup shortening
1 cup sugar
2 eggs, well beaten
2 cups all-purpose flour
1 tsp. baking powder
⅛ tsp. salt
½ cup milk
2 tsp. lemon juice
1 tsp. grated lemon rind
½ cup walnuts

Glaze
2 tsp. sugar
2 tsp. grated lemon rind
1 tsp. lemon juice

Preheat the oven to 300°.

In a large bowl, cream together the shortening and sugar, mixing well. Add the eggs and beat well again.

In another bowl, mix together 1 cup of the flour, baking powder, and salt and then add that mixture to the creamed mixture, blending well to incorporate. Next, blend in the milk, lemon juice, lemon rind, and walnuts. Add the remaining 1 cup of flour and mix well again. Pour the batter into a well-greased loaf pan and bake for 90 minutes.

For glaze: Mix together the sugar, lemon rind, and lemon juice. (You may need a few more drops of lemon juice if the mixture is too thick.) When the bread is done, spread the glaze on top of the loaf and let cool.

Notes:

46 No-Knead Oatmeal Bread

2 to 2½ cups all-purpose flour
¾ cup rolled oats
1 tsp. salt
2¼ tsp. (1 package) active dry yeast
1 cup water
¼ cup molasses
¼ cup (½ stick) butter
1 egg

In a large bowl, combine 1 cup of the flour, rolled oats, salt, and yeast; blend well.

In a small saucepan, heat the water, molasses, and butter to quite warm (120° to 130°). Add the warm liquid and the egg to the flour mixture. Using an electric mixer, blend at low speed until the flour mixture is incorporated; then turn the mixer to medium speed and continue mixing for 3 minutes. Stir in an additional 1 to 1½ cups of the flour to form a stiff batter. Cover the bowl with a towel and let the batter rise in a warm place until doubled, about 45 to 60 minutes.

Stir down the batter and then pour it into a greased loaf pan. Cover and let it rise until the batter reaches the top of the pan, about 30 minutes, although you'll want to watch carefully so it doesn't rise too high.

Preheat the oven to 375° and bake for 35 to 40 minutes or until done. Remove the bread from the pan immediately and cool on a wire rack.

Notes:

47 Oatmeal Bread

2 cups milk, scalded and cooled slightly
2 cups rolled oats, plus extra for sprinkling the bread tops
½ cup brown sugar
2 T. shortening
1 T. salt
2¼ tsp. (1 package) active dry yeast
½ cup warm water (about 110°)
5 cups all-purpose flour, more or less
1 egg white
1 T. water

Stir together the scalded milk, 2 cups rolled oats, brown sugar, shortening, and salt.

In a large mixing bowl, sprinkle the yeast on the warm water. Let it stand for 5 minutes. Add the milk mixture and 2 cups of the flour. Beat with a spoon until the batter is smooth. Add enough remaining flour, a little at a time, until the dough becomes soft and leaves the sides of the bowl. Turn onto a floured work surface and knead for about 8 minutes.

Place the dough ball in a lightly greased bowl, turning the dough so the entire surface is greased. Let it stand, covered, in a warm place until doubled, about 1 hour. Punch down and return the dough to the greased bowl, turning the dough so the entire surface is greased; cover and let it rise a second time until nearly doubled, about 40 minutes.

Turn out the dough onto a lightly floured surface and make 2 balls of dough. Cover and let the dough rest for 10 minutes. Shape into loaves

Notes:

and place in 2 greased loaf pans. Let loaves rise until almost doubled, about 1 hour.

Preheat the oven to 375°.

Beat the egg white with 1 tablespoon of water, and brush the tops of the loaves with the egg mixture. Sprinkle the tops with rolled oats.

Bake for 40 minutes or until done.

---

48 Pumpkin Whole Wheat Quick Bread

3 cups brown sugar
5 cups whole wheat flour
1 tsp. cinnamon
½ tsp. cloves
1 tsp. salt
1 heaping T. baking soda
1 cup cooking oil
2½ cups canned pumpkin
2 eggs

Preheat the oven to 350°.

In a large bowl and using a large wooden spoon, mix together the brown sugar, flour, cinnamon, cloves, salt, and baking soda. Add the oil, canned pumpkin, and eggs and mix again. When thoroughly blended, divide the dough between 2 greased loaf pans.

Bake for about 1 hour and 20 minutes or until done.

Notes:

49 Quick Garlic Cheese Breadsticks

½ cup (1 stick) butter, melted
2½ cups all-purpose flour
4 tsp. baking powder
1⅓ cups milk
2 tsp. garlic powder
Parmesan cheese to taste
dried parsley (optional)

Preheat the oven to 450°.

Pour the melted butter into a 9 x 13-inch baking pan. In a large mixing bowl, mix together the flour, baking powder, and milk and stir until a soft dough forms. Knead about 3 minutes, adding extra flour if the dough is too sticky.

Roll out the dough to form a rectangle that is 8 inches wide and ½ an inch high. Cut width-wise into strips about 1½ inches wide. Place the strips into the pan and turn them so both sides are buttered. Sprinkle the strips with the garlic powder, Parmesan cheese, and parsley.

Bake for 15 to 20 minutes or until done.

Notes:

50 Rustic Baking Soda Bread

¾ cup (1½ sticks) butter, divided
1¼ cups buttermilk, divided
4 cups all-purpose flour
¼ cup sugar
1 tsp. baking soda
1 T. baking powder
½ tsp. salt
1 egg

Preheat the oven to 375°. Grease a large baking sheet and set aside.

Melt ¼ cup of the butter and, in a small bowl, mix it together with ¼ cup of the buttermilk; set aside.

In a large bowl, mix together the flour, sugar, baking soda, baking powder, salt, and ½ cup butter, softened to room temperature. Stir in 1 cup of buttermilk and the egg. Turn the dough out onto a lightly floured surface and knead lightly for about 45 seconds. Form the dough into a round and place it on the prepared baking sheet. Cut an *X* on the top of the loaf and then brush with the melted butter mixture.

Bake for 45 to 50 minutes or until a toothpick inserted into the center of the loaf comes out clean. (Start checking for doneness at about 35 minutes.) During baking, you can continue to brush the top of the loaf with the melted butter mixture, and then brush the top of the loaf one more time as soon as it comes from the oven.

Notes:

51 Rustic Peasant Bread

2¼ tsp. (1 package) active dry yeast
1 T. sugar
2 tsp. salt
2 cups warm water (about 110°)
1 T. oil, plus more for brushing the top of the loaf (olive oil
    tastes great in this recipe)
4½ cups all-purpose flour

BREADS
(YEAST AND QUICK)

Mix together the yeast, sugar, and salt; add the warm water and mix together; add the oil. Add the flour a cup at a time, incorporating well after each addition; knead the dough until smooth, about 5 to 7 minutes. Place the dough in a greased bowl and cover. Let it rise for 30 minutes.

Form the dough into a round loaf and place it on a greased cookie sheet. Cover and let it rise again, about 45 minutes.

Brush the top of the loaf with oil, and bake in a preheated oven at 425° for 10 minutes; reduce the heat to 375°; brush again with oil, and continue baking for 20 more minutes.

Notes:

52 Rye and Dill Bread

3½ to 4 cups all-purpose flour
1½ cups rye flour
½ cup instant milk powder
4½ tsp. (2 packages) active dry
    yeast
2 tsp. sugar

1 tsp. salt
1 tsp. caraway seeds
1 tsp. dill seeds
1 tsp. dill weed
2¾ cups water
2 tsp. shortening

In a large bowl, mix together 2 cups all-purpose flour, the rye flour, milk powder, yeast, sugar, salt, caraway seeds, dill seeds, and dill weed.

In a saucepan, heat together the water and shortening until it reaches 120° to 130°. Add the liquid to the flour mixture and beat for 3 minutes. Stir in enough remaining all-purpose flour to form a soft dough that pulls away from the sides of the bowl.

Turn out the dough onto a floured work surface and knead for 8 minutes. Place the dough into a greased bowl, turning the dough so the entire surface is greased. Cover and let it rise until doubled, about 1 hour.

Punch down the dough and let it rest, covered, on a lightly floured surface for about 10 minutes. Divide the dough in half and form 2 round loaves. Place the loaves onto 2 greased baking sheets, cover, and let the bread rise for about 35 to 45 minutes.

When ready to bake, make 3 shallow slashes across the top of each loaf with a sharp knife. Bake in a preheated 375° oven for 30 to 35 minutes or until done, exchanging position of the pans halfway through baking if the pans are on separate racks in the oven.

Notes:

53 Rye Bread

4 cups all-purpose flour
2 cups rye flour
4½ tsp. (2 packages) active dry yeast
1½ tsp. salt
2 T. caraway seeds
2 cups buttermilk
⅓ cup molasses
⅓ cup butter
2 T. melted butter

In a medium bowl, mix together the all-purpose flour and rye flour. In a large mixing bowl, combine 2 cups of the mixed flour, yeast, salt, and caraway seeds.

Heat the buttermilk, molasses, and ⅓ cup butter in a saucepan over low heat until warm (about 120°). The butter won't be entirely melted, and the mixture may look curdled, which is okay. Pour the liquid into the flour and yeast mixture and beat for about 3 minutes on medium speed. Add another ½ cup of the flour mixture and continue beating for 2 minutes more. With a large wooden spoon, stir in enough additional flour to make a soft dough.

Turn the dough out onto a floured work surface and knead for 10 minutes. Shape the dough into a ball and place it into a greased bowl, turning the dough so the entire surface is greased. Cover and let it rise until double, about 1½ hours.

Punch down the dough and then turn out onto a lightly floured surface. Cut in half, cover the dough, and let it rest for 15 minutes. Shape

Notes:

each piece into a ball and place the balls of dough on a greased cookie sheet. (You may need to use two cookie sheets if you don't have a large size.) Cover the dough and let it rise again until double, about 1 hour.

Preheat the oven to 350°. Brush the loaves with 2 tablespoons melted butter and bake 35 minutes or until done, rotating the cookie sheets halfway through baking if using two. Remove the pan from the oven and allow the loaves to cool on wire racks.

54 Soy Flour Bread

2¼ tsp. (1 package) active dry yeast
½ cup warm water (about 120°)
pinch of sugar
2 cups warm milk or water (about 120°)
1 T. shortening
1 tsp. salt
1 T. sugar
2 cups soy flour
4 cups all-purpose flour, plus more for kneading

Dissolve the yeast in warm water to which you have added a pinch of sugar. Let it stand about 10 minutes or until bubbly.

In a large bowl, mix together the warm milk, shortening, salt, and sugar. Add the yeast mixture and then gradually add the soy flour, mixing as you go. Beat for about 2 to 3 minutes. Gradually add the all-purpose flour (you'll probably need to use a large wooden spoon when the dough gets thick) until it forms a loose ball and pulls away from the sides of the bowl. Turn out the dough onto a floured work surface and knead until smooth and elastic, about 8 minutes.

Notes:

67

Place the ball of dough into a large greased bowl, turning the dough so the entire surface is greased. Cover and set in a warm place to rise until double, about 2 hours.

Divide the dough in half and shape into loaves. Place in greased loaf pans, cover, and let rise until the bread reaches about an inch above the top of the pan, about 45 minutes.

Bake in a preheated 375° oven for 35 to 40 minutes or until done.

- -

55 Whole Wheat Bread

2 to 2½ cups warm water (about 120°)
4½ tsp. (2 packages) active dry yeast
½ cup cooking oil
½ cup honey (you can also use molasses)
½ cup nonfat dry milk powder
2½ tsp. salt
7 cups whole wheat flour, more or less

Pour ½ cup of the warm water into a large bowl and sprinkle the yeast on top. Allow to sit for about 10 minutes or until the mixture bubbles. Add the remaining warm water, oil, honey, milk powder, salt, and about half of the flour. Beat for about 3 minutes to develop the gluten (you can also beat by hand using a large wooden spoon), and then gradually add more flour, beating well after each addition, until a soft dough forms and begins to pull away from the sides of the bowl.

Turn out the dough onto a floured work surface and knead, adding flour as needed to prevent sticking, for 10 minutes. (The less flour you use, the softer your bread will be.)

Notes:

Place the dough ball into a large, well-greased bowl, turning the dough so the entire surface is greased. Cover the bowl and let the dough rise until double, about 1½ to 2 hours.

Punch down the dough, knead again for a minute or so, and then place it back in the greased bowl, turning the dough so the entire surface is greased. Cover with a towel and let the dough rise again until nearly double, about 1 to 1½ hours.

Punch down the dough and shape it into 2 loaves. Place the loaves into 2 greased loaf pans, cover, and let the dough rise until it reaches about 1 inch above the tops of the pans, about an hour.

Bake in a preheated 375° oven for 40 to 45 minutes or until done.

Notes:

56 Zucchini Bread

3 eggs
1¾ cups sugar
2 cups grated zucchini
1 cup (2 sticks) butter, melted and cooled slightly
2 tsp. vanilla
3 cups all-purpose flour
2½ tsp. cinnamon
½ tsp. nutmeg
1 tsp. baking soda
½ tsp. baking powder
1 tsp. salt
1 cup walnuts
½ cup raisins, optional

BREADS (YEAST AND QUICK)

Preheat the oven to 325°. In a large bowl, mix together the eggs and sugar. Add the grated zucchini, melted butter, and vanilla, and stir to mix well.

In another large bowl, whisk together the flour, cinnamon, nutmeg, baking soda, baking powder, and salt.

Add the flour mixture to the egg mixture and mix just until blended. (Don't overmix.) Blend in the nuts and raisins (if using). Pour the batter into 2 greased loaf pans and bake for 60 to 70 minutes or until done. Let the zucchini bread sit for 10 minutes and then take the loaves out of the pans and place on wire racks to cool completely.

Notes:

MUFFINS

Muffins are one of the workhorses in your kitchen recipe collection. They are quick and easy to prepare, and the taste variations are almost endless. You can make sweet or savory muffins, and eat them for breakfast, lunch, dinner, snacks, or dessert. Pretty much any time of the day is muffin time.

Muffins freeze well too, so they make a great last-minute take-along breakfast or snack when heading out the door in the morning. Simply freeze muffins in individual baggies and grab a bag to go—just one example of old-fashioned "fast food."

Some folks use paper cupcake holders to bake their muffins in, but I admit to being too frugal for that. Instead, I bake my muffins in well-greased muffin tins, and they slip right out after baking. I remove them from the muffin cups and cool them on wire racks so the bottoms don't get soggy.

Some of our favorites include Blueberry Oatmeal Muffins, Chocolate Chip Muffins, and popovers. And then there are the traditional standbys, such as cornmeal muffins and Four-Week Refrigerator Bran Muffins. And don't forget to try some of the savory muffins, like our Bacon and Cheddar Cheese Muffins. Whichever recipes you try, I think you'll agree that muffins are a tasty way to satisfy your family's hunger pangs.

Whatever you do, work at it with all your heart,
as working for the Lord, not for human masters,
since you know that you will receive an inheritance
from the Lord as a reward.
It is the Lord Christ you are serving.

COLOSSIANS 3:23-24

Lord Jesus, please help me to choose each and every day
to do my work cheerfully and with all of my heart. On
those days when my daily duties seem never-ending and
unappreciated, help me remember that I'm working
for You, Lord, first and foremost. Remind me that You
are pleased when I work in service for others for Your
name's sake. Turn my thoughts back to You, and renew
a right spirit within me. Bless Your holy name! Amen.

57 Apple Pumpkin Muffins with Streusel Topping

Muffins
2½ cups all-purpose flour
2 cups sugar
1 T. pumpkin pie spice
1 tsp. baking soda
½ tsp. salt
2 eggs
¾ cup cooked pumpkin (or use canned pumpkin)
½ cup cooking oil
2 cups apples, peeled and finely chopped

Streusel Topping
2 T. flour
¼ cup sugar
½ tsp. cinnamon
2 tsp. butter, softened

Preheat the oven to 350°.

In a large bowl, mix together the flour, sugar, pumpkin pie spice, baking soda, and salt. In another bowl, beat together the eggs, pumpkin, and cooking oil. Add to the dry ingredients and stir until just blended. Don't overmix. Stir in the apples. Fill greased muffin cups about ¾ full.

For topping: Mix together the flour, sugar, and cinnamon; add the butter and mix until combined. Sprinkle on top of the muffins.

Bake for 30 to 35 minutes or until done. Remove the muffins from the pan and cool on a wire rack.

Note: This makes quite a large batch, so you may have to bake in shifts.

MUFFINS

Notes:

58 Bacon and Cheddar Cheese Muffins

2 cups all-purpose flour
2 T. sugar
3 tsp. baking powder
½ tsp. salt
½ cup cooked, crumbled bacon
½ cup Cheddar cheese
¼ cup finely diced onions (optional)
1 cup milk
1 egg, beaten
¼ cup (½ stick) butter, melted and cooled to lukewarm

Preheat the oven to 425°.

In a large bowl, whisk together the flour, sugar, baking powder, and salt. Add the bacon, cheese, and onions (if using) and mix again. Make a well in the center of the flour mixture.

In a small bowl, mix together the milk, egg, and melted butter. Pour this mixture all at once into the well and stir just until moistened. Do not overmix.

Fill greased muffin cups ⅔ full and bake for 20 to 25 minutes or until done. Immediately remove the muffins from the pan and place on a wire rack to cool.

Notes:

MUFFINS

59 Berry Muffins

1¾ cups all-purpose flour
1 cup plus 2 T. sugar, divided
2½ tsp. baking powder
½ tsp. cinnamon
¼ tsp. salt
1 cup milk
¼ cup (½ stick) butter, melted
1 egg, beaten
1 tsp. vanilla
1 cup berries, fresh or frozen (blueberries, blackberries,
    cranberries...)

Preheat the oven to 375°.

In a large bowl, whisk together the flour, 1 cup of the sugar, baking powder, cinnamon, and salt.

In another bowl, stir together the milk, butter, egg, and vanilla. Add to the dry ingredients and stir just until blended. Do not overmix. Fold in the berries.

Fill greased muffin cups ¾ full. Sprinkle with the remaining 2 tablespoons sugar. Bake for 20 minutes or until done. Remove the muffins from the pan and cool on a wire rack.

Notes:

60 Blueberry Oatmeal Muffins

1 cup all-purpose flour
2 tsp. baking powder
½ tsp. salt
½ tsp. cinnamon
½ cup brown sugar
¾ cup rolled oats
1 egg
1 cup milk
¼ cup (½ stick) butter, melted
¾ cup blueberries, fresh or frozen
sugar or cinnamon sugar for sprinkling

Preheat the oven to 375°.

Whisk together the flour, baking powder, salt, and cinnamon. Add the brown sugar and rolled oats and mix well.

In a large bowl, beat together the egg, milk, and melted butter. Add the dry ingredients and stir just until blended. Do not overmix. Fold in the blueberries.

Fill greased muffin cups ⅔ full and sprinkle some sugar (or cinnamon sugar) on top of each muffin. Bake for 20 minutes or until done. Remove the muffins from the pan and cool on a wire rack.

Notes:

MUFFINS

61 Bran Muffins

1 cup All-Bran cereal
1 cup milk
2 T. shortening
¼ cup sugar
1 egg, well beaten
1 cup all-purpose flour
3 tsp. baking powder
½ tsp. salt

Preheat the oven to 400°.

In a medium bowl, mix together the bran cereal and milk and let stand for 5 minutes.

In a large bowl, cream together the shortening and sugar. Add the beaten egg and beat until smooth. Add the bran mixture.

In another bowl whisk together the flour, baking powder, and salt. Add to the bran mixture and mix just until blended. Do not overmix.

Fill greased muffin cups ⅔ full and bake for 25 minutes or until done. Remove the muffins from the pan and cool on a wire rack.

MUFFINS

Notes:

62 Cheese Muffins

2 cups all-purpose flour
1 T. sugar
3 tsp. baking powder
½ tsp. salt
¾ cup shredded Cheddar cheese
1 cup milk
1 egg, beaten
¼ cup (½ stick) butter, melted

Preheat the oven to 425°.

In a large bowl, whisk together the flour, sugar, baking powder, and salt. Add the cheese and stir to mix.

In a medium bowl, mix together the milk, egg, and melted butter. Make a well in the center of the flour mixture and pour the liquid mixture all at once into the well. Stir just until moistened. Do not overmix.

Fill greased muffin cups ⅔ full and bake for 20 to 25 minutes or until done. Remove the muffins from the pan and cool on a wire rack.

MUFFINS

Notes:

63 Chocolate Chip Muffins

1½ cups all-purpose flour
½ cup sugar
2 tsp. baking powder
½ tsp. salt
1 egg
½ cup milk
¼ cup cooking oil
¾ cup chocolate chips

Preheat the oven to 400°.

In a large bowl, whisk together the flour, sugar, baking powder, and salt.

In another bowl, beat the egg and then add it to the flour mixture along with the milk and cooking oil. Stir just until blended. Don't overmix. Gently fold in the chocolate chips.

Fill greased muffins cups about ⅔ full. Bake for 20 to 25 minutes or until done. Remove the muffins from the pan and cool on a wire rack.

Notes:

64 Chocolate Coffee Muffins

Frosting
4 ounces cream cheese, cubed
1 T. sugar
½ tsp. instant coffee granules
¼ cup semisweet chocolate mini chips

Muffins
2 cups all-purpose flour
¾ cup sugar
2½ tsp. baking powder
1 tsp. cinnamon
½ tsp. salt
1 cup milk
2 T. instant coffee granules
½ cup (1 stick) butter, melted
1 egg
1 tsp. vanilla
¾ cup semisweet chocolate mini chips

Preheat the oven to 375°.

For frosting: In a medium bowl, beat together the frosting ingredients until mostly smooth (the chocolate chips will break down into smaller pieces). Alternately, you can use a food processor if you have one to make a smoother spread. Cover the bowl and refrigerate the frosting until ready to use.

For muffins: In a large bowl, mix together the flour, sugar, baking powder, cinnamon, and salt.

Notes:

In a medium bowl, stir the milk and coffee granules until the coffee is dissolved. Add the melted butter, egg, and vanilla and stir to mix well. Stir the liquid mixture into the flour mixture just until moistened. Use a rubber spatula and fold in the chocolate chips.

Grease muffin cups and fill about ⅔ full with batter. (You may need two pans.) Bake for 17 to 20 minutes or until done. Cool for 5 minutes and then remove the muffins from the pan to a wire rack. When the muffins are barely warm, spread the frosting on the tops.

- -

65 Cornmeal Muffins

1 cup all-purpose flour
1 cup cornmeal
3 T. sugar
3 tsp. baking powder
½ tsp. salt
1 cup milk
1 egg, beaten
¼ cup (½ stick) butter, melted

Preheat the oven to 425°.

In a large bowl, whisk together the flour, cornmeal, sugar, baking powder, and salt.

In a medium bowl, mix together the milk, egg, and melted butter. Make a well in the center of the flour mixture and then add the liquid mixture all at once into the well. Stir just until moistened. Do not overmix.

Fill greased muffin cups ⅔ full and bake for 20 to 25 minutes or until done.

Notes:

66 Four-Week Refrigerator Bran Muffins

6 cups ready-to-eat bran cereal, divided
2 cups boiling water
1 cup shortening or butter
1½ cups sugar
4 eggs
1 quart buttermilk
5 cups all-purpose flour
5 tsp. baking soda
1 tsp. salt
raisins, dates, dried fruit, or nuts (optional)

Place 2 cups of the bran cereal into a medium bowl and pour in the boiling water. Set aside to cool. Meanwhile, in a large bowl, cream together the shortening or butter, sugar, and eggs. Add the buttermilk and the cooled cereal mixture.

In a large bowl, whisk together the flour, baking soda, and salt and add to the creamed mixture. Stir until the flour is blended. Fold in the remaining 4 cups of dry bran cereal and the dried fruit or nuts, if using.

Store the batter in a covered container in the refrigerator for up to 4 weeks.

To use: When ready to bake the muffins, preheat the oven to 400° and fill well-greased muffin cups ⅔ full. Bake for 20 minutes or until done. Remove the muffins from the pan and cool on a wire rack.

MUFFINS

Notes:

67 Ginger Muffins

¼ cup shortening
¼ cup sugar
1 egg
½ cup molasses
1½ cups all-purpose flour
¾ tsp. baking soda
¼ tsp. salt
½ tsp. cinnamon
½ tsp. ground ginger
¼ tsp. ground cloves
¼ cup bran
½ cup buttermilk

Preheat the oven to 375°.

In a large bowl, cream together the shortening and sugar. Beat in the egg and then the molasses.

In another large bowl, whisk together the flour, baking soda, salt, cinnamon, ginger, cloves, and bran. Stir the flour mixture into the molasses mixture and then gradually add the buttermilk, beating until smooth.

Fill greased muffin cups ⅔ full and bake for 20 to 25 minutes or until done. Remove the muffins from the pan and cool on a wire rack.

68 Honey Muffins

2 cups all-purpose flour
½ cup sugar
3 tsp. baking powder
½ tsp. salt
1 egg
1 cup milk
¼ cup (½ stick) butter, melted
¼ cup honey

Preheat the oven to 400°.

In a large bowl, mix together the flour, sugar, baking powder, and salt.

In a small bowl, mix together the egg, milk, butter, and honey. Stir this mixture into the flour mixture just until moistened. Don't overmix.

Fill greased muffin cups about ⅔ full and bake for 15 to 18 minutes or until done. Cool in the pan for 5 minutes and then remove the muffins to cool on a wire rack. (These muffins, however, are best eaten warm.)

Notes:

69 Jam Muffins

2 cups all-purpose flour
3 T. sugar
3 tsp. baking powder
½ tsp. salt
1 cup milk
1 egg, beaten
¼ cup (½ stick) butter, melted
6 tsp. jam (you can use more if you desire)

Preheat the oven to 425°.

In a large bowl, whisk together the flour, sugar, baking powder, and salt.

In a medium bowl, mix together the milk, egg, and melted butter. Make a well in the center of the flour mixture and then add the liquid mixture all at once into the well. Stir just until moistened. Do not overmix.

Fill greased muffin cups ⅔ full; add ½ tsp. jam (or a bit more if you desire) to the top of each muffin, and bake for 20 to 25 minutes or until done. Remove the muffins from the pan and cool on a wire rack.

MUFFINS

Notes:

70 Lemon Muffins

2 cups all-purpose flour
3 tsp. baking powder
½ tsp. salt
1 box instant lemon pudding mix
2 T. sugar
1⅓ cups milk
¼ cup cooking oil
powdered sugar for sprinkling

Preheat the oven to 425°.

In a large bowl, whisk together the flour, baking powder, salt, pudding mix, and sugar. In another bowl, mix together the milk and cooking oil and pour it into the flour mixture, stirring just until blended. Do not overmix.

Fill greased muffin cups ⅔ full and bake for 20 to 25 minutes or until done. Remove from the oven and place them on a wire rack to cool. Sprinkle with powdered sugar if desired.

MUFFINS

Notes:

71 Lemon Muffins for a Crowd

Muffins
6 cups all-purpose flour
4 cups sugar
¾ tsp. baking soda
¾ tsp. salt
8 eggs
2 cups sour cream
2 cups (4 sticks) butter, melted
3 T. grated lemon peel
2 T. lemon juice

Crumb Topping
¾ cup all-purpose flour
¾ cup sugar
¼ cup (½ stick) very cold
    butter, cubed

Glaze
½ cup sugar
⅓ cup lemon juice

For muffins: Preheat the oven to 350°.

In a large bowl, whisk together the flour, sugar, baking soda, and salt.

In another large bowl, mix together the eggs, sour cream, melted butter, lemon peel, and lemon juice. Stir into the flour mixture just until moistened. Don't over-stir.

For crumb topping: In a small bowl, combine the flour and sugar; cut in the butter until the mixture resembles coarse crumbles.

Getting ready to bake: Fill greased muffin cups about ⅔ full. (You'll need around 40 cups if you plan to bake them all at once. Or, you can keep the batter in the refrigerator and bake in batches.) Sprinkle the crumb topping over the batter in the muffin tins.

Bake for 20 to 25 minutes or until done. Cool in the pans for 5 minutes; then remove the muffins to wire racks to cool.

For glaze: Mix together the sugar and lemon juice and drizzle the glaze over the muffins while they are still warm.

MUFFINS

Notes:

72 Maple Crumb Muffins

Muffins

2 cups all-purpose flour
½ cup brown sugar
2 tsp. baking powder
½ tsp. salt
¾ cup milk

½ cup (1 stick) butter, melted
½ cup maple syrup
¼ cup sour cream
1 egg
½ tsp. vanilla

Crumb Topping

3 T. all-purpose flour
3 T. sugar
2 T. finely chopped walnuts or pecans
½ tsp. cinnamon
2 T. (¼ stick) very cold butter, cubed

For muffins: Preheat the oven to 400°. In a large bowl, mix together the flour, brown sugar, baking powder, and salt.

In another bowl, combine the milk, melted butter, maple syrup, sour cream, egg, and vanilla. Stir into the flour mixture just until moistened. Don't overmix.

For crumb topping: Mix together the flour, sugar, nuts, and cinnamon; cut in the butter until the mixture resembles coarse crumbles.

Getting ready to bake: Fill greased muffin cups about ⅔ full with batter. Sprinkle the crumb topping over the tops of the muffins.

Bake for 16 to 20 minutes until done. Cool for 5 minutes before removing muffins from the pan to a wire rack to cool.

Notes:

73 Oatmeal, Apple, and Raisin Muffins

1 egg
¾ cup milk
½ cup cooking oil
1 cup uncooked rolled oats
1 cup chopped apples
1 cup raisins
1 cup all-purpose flour
⅓ cup sugar
3 tsp. baking powder
1 tsp. salt
1 tsp. nutmeg
2 tsp. cinnamon

Preheat the oven to 400°.

In a large bowl, beat the egg; add the milk and oil and stir until mixed. Add the remaining ingredients and stir just until blended. Do not overmix. Fill greased muffin cups about ¾ full.

Bake for 15 to 20 minutes or until done. Remove the muffins from the pan and cool on a wire rack.

MUFFINS

Notes:

74 Orange Muffins

2 cups all-purpose flour
½ cup sugar
3 T. baking powder
½ tsp. salt
1 T. grated orange peel
¾ cup milk
¼ cup orange juice
1 egg, beaten
¼ cup (½ stick) butter, melted

Preheat the oven to 425°.

In a large bowl, whisk together the flour, sugar, baking powder, salt, and orange peel.

In a medium bowl, mix together the milk, orange juice, egg, and melted butter.

Make a well in the center of the flour mixture and then add the liquid mixture all at once into the well. Stir just until moistened. Do not overmix.

Fill greased muffin cups ⅔ full and bake for 20 to 25 minutes or until done. Remove the muffins from the pan and cool on a wire rack.

Notes:

MUFFINS

75 Popovers

1 cup flour
¼ tsp. salt (I usually go a little heavy on the salt)
1 tsp. sugar (optional—we don't use sugar because we eat our
     popovers as a savory side to our meal, but cook's choice)
1 T. butter, melted and cooled
1 cup milk
2 eggs

Preheat the oven to 375°. Grease or butter 10 ½-cup custard cups or muffin cups.

In a mixing bowl, stir together the flour, salt, and sugar, if you're using it. Mix thoroughly. Add the butter, milk, and eggs; beat until the batter is very smooth, about 2½ minutes, remembering to scrape the sides often. (My original recipe called for using an electric mixer, but I now use my lovely, Amish-made, hand-cranked egg beaters, which work just as well, but beating as fast as I can for several minutes is quite an upper arm workout!)

Fill the prepared custard cups or muffin cups about halfway, and bake on the center rack of your oven for 50 to 55 minutes.

Note: Like a soufflé, popovers wait for no one. When you bring them from the oven to the table, they will begin to deflate as they cool. So be prepared to have everyone at the table and ready to eat when the buzzer goes off.

MUFFINS

Notes:

76 Raisin Muffins

2 cups all-purpose flour
3 T. sugar
3 tsp. baking powder
½ tsp. salt
½ to ¾ cup raisins
1 cup milk
1 egg, beaten
¼ cup (½ stick) butter, melted

Preheat the oven to 425°.

In a large bowl, whisk together the flour, sugar, baking powder, and salt. Add the raisins and mix.

In a medium bowl, mix together the milk, egg, and melted butter. Make a well in the center of the flour mixture and then add the liquid mixture all at once into the well. Stir just until moistened. Do not overmix.

Fill greased muffin cups ⅔ full and bake for 20 to 25 minutes or until done. Remove the muffins from the pan and cool on a wire rack.

MUFFINS

Notes:

77 Rhubarb Muffins

Muffins
1½ cups all-purpose flour
1 cup whole wheat flour
1 tsp. baking soda
1 tsp. baking powder
½ tsp. salt
1 cup buttermilk or plain yogurt
¾ cup brown sugar
½ cup cooking oil
1 egg, beaten
2 tsp. vanilla
1½ cups diced rhubarb

Topping
¼ cup sugar
1 T. butter, melted
1 tsp. cinnamon
1 tsp. flour

For muffins: Preheat the oven to 375°.

In a medium bowl, whisk together the all-purpose flour, whole wheat flour, baking soda, baking powder, and salt.

In a large bowl, combine the buttermilk (or yogurt), brown sugar, cooking oil, beaten egg, and vanilla. Fold in the rhubarb. Fill greased muffin cups ⅔ full.

For topping: Mix together the sugar, melted butter, cinnamon, and flour. Sprinkle on top of the muffins.

Bake for 20 minutes or until done. Remove the muffins from the pan and cool on a wire rack.

Notes:

78 Summer Peach Muffins

1 cup peeled and chopped fresh peaches
1 tsp. lemon juice
⅔ cup sugar
½ tsp. salt
¼ tsp. cinnamon
3 tsp. baking powder
1 cup milk
1 egg
¼ cup (½ stick) butter, melted
2 cups all-purpose flour

In a small bowl, sprinkle the peaches with the lemon juice and mix to cover the pieces; set aside.

In a large bowl, mix together the sugar, salt, cinnamon, and baking powder. Add the milk, egg, and butter and mix well. Add the flour and mix again, being careful to not overmix. Fold in the fruit and then fill greased muffin cups ⅔ full.

Bake for 20 minutes or until done. Remove the muffins from the pan and cool on a wire rack.

Notes:

ROLLS AND BUNS

Generally, rolls and buns take a bit more time from start to finish, but the results are definitely worth the effort. They are good any day of the week, but will shine when part of a special meal. Rolls and buns just seem to say, "Celebrate!"

Even if you are a seasoned bread baker, you may not have tried expanding your repertoire to include the recipes in this section. But do give them a try, and once you do, the next step is to play around with the ingredients. Use different types of flour. Add some of this or a pinch of that—just use what's available or what seems like a good addition to the recipe. You may be pleasantly surprised with the results, and you just might "unvent" (because there's nothing new under the sun!) a new family favorite.

Try the mashed potato rolls, hamburger buns, or the Overnight Refrigerator Butter Crescent Rolls (they don't need kneading!) to get started. If I don't miss my guess, you'll wonder why you would ever eat store-bought rolls or buns again. They are that good!

*Godliness with contentment is great gain...
and having food and raiment let
us be therewith content.*

1 Timothy 6:6,8 kjv

---

*Heavenly Father, I want to experience that great
gain You speak of in Your Word—godliness
with contentment in whatever circumstances I
am in. Remind me often that contentment has
nothing to do with how easy my life might be, and
everything to do with the state of my heart. May
my heart constantly be tuned to You. Amen.*

79 Black Raspberry Sweet Rolls

Rolls
3½ to 4 cups all-purpose flour
½ cup sugar
1 tsp. salt
4½ tsp. (2 packages) active dry yeast
1 cup milk
½ cup butter (1 stick)
2 eggs

Topping
¼ cup (½ stick) butter, melted
½ cup black raspberry preserves (you can also use red raspberry,
    blackberry, etc.)

Glaze
1 cup powdered sugar
2 to 3 T. milk

For rolls: In a large bowl, whisk together 1½ cups flour with the sugar, salt, and yeast.

In a small saucepan, heat 1 cup milk and ½ cup butter until about 115°; pour the milk mixture into the flour mixture and blend on low speed until incorporated. Add the eggs and blend again, and then beat the dough on medium speed for 3 minutes. Gradually stir in additional flour (about 2 cups should do it) until the dough pulls away from the sides of the bowl.

Turn out the dough on a floured work surface and knead for about 4 to 5 minutes, adding small amounts of flour as needed to keep the dough from sticking. Place the dough in a large greased bowl, turning

Notes:

the dough so the entire surface is greased. Cover and let rise until double, about an hour.

Punch down the dough and then turn out onto a lightly floured work surface. Divide the dough into 24 pieces. Roll each piece into a 15-inch rope.

Grease cookie sheets (you will probably need 3 total) and, working directly on the prepared cookie sheet, loosely coil each rope into a circle, tucking the ends underneath. Cover and let the rolls rise until double, about 20 to 30 minutes. Meanwhile, preheat the oven to 350°.

For topping: When ready to bake, gently brush the rolls with ¼ cup melted butter (save the leftover butter to use after baking); make a deep indent with your thumb or knuckle in the center of each roll. Spoon about 1 teaspoon of the black raspberry preserves into each thumbprint.

Bake for about 15 to 20 minutes or until done and the tops are a light golden brown; remove from the cookie sheets immediately and brush a second time with the leftover melted butter. Allow the rolls to cool.

For glaze: Mix together the powdered sugar and milk and then drizzle the glaze over the cooled rolls.

Notes:

80 Butter Pan Rolls

4½ tsp. (2 packages) active dry yeast
½ cup warm water (about 110°)
4½ cups all-purpose flour
¼ cup sugar
1 tsp. salt
1 cup (2 sticks) plus 2 T. (¼ stick) butter, melted and cooled
1 egg, beaten
1 cup warm milk (about 110°)

In a medium bowl, dissolve the yeast in the warm water; allow to stand until bubbly, about 10 to 15 minutes.

In a large bowl, whisk together 2 cups of the flour with the sugar and salt. Add 6 tablespoons of the melted butter, the egg, the yeast mixture, and the warm milk. Beat for 5 minutes on medium speed.

Gradually beat in the remaining flour. Cover the bowl and let the batter rise until doubled, about 45 minutes to an hour.

Pour half of the remaining butter into a 9 x 13-inch baking pan, making sure to coat the entire bottom of the pan. (You may need to re-liquefy the butter and then cool it again to barely warm.) Beat down the batter and then drop by spoonfuls into the buttered pan. (Makes about 15 rolls.) Drizzle the remaining butter over the dough. Cover loosely with plastic wrap and let the dough rise again until almost doubled, about 30 minutes. Meanwhile, preheat the oven to 425°.

Bake the rolls for 12 to 17 minutes or until done.

Notes:

81 Butterscotch Rolls

Bottom of Pans
½ cup (1 stick) butter, melted
1½ cups brown sugar

Rolls
2½ cups all-purpose or pastry flour
3½ tsp. baking powder
1 tsp. salt
¼ cup sugar
5 T. shortening
½ cup milk
1 egg, well beaten

Preheat the oven to 400°.

For pans: Lightly grease 24 muffin cups. Put 1 teaspoon melted butter and 1 teaspoon brown sugar into the bottom of each muffin cup. You won't use all of the melted butter and brown sugar; the rest will be spread on the dough (see below).

For rolls: In a large bowl, whisk together the flour, baking powder, salt, and sugar. Cut in the shortening until it resembles coarse crumbles.

In a small bowl, mix together the milk and egg; add to the flour mixture and stir until mixed. Turn out onto a floured surface and knead 20 times. Roll the dough into an oblong shape ¼ inch thick. Spread the remaining melted butter on the dough and then sprinkle with the remaining brown sugar. Roll up the dough jelly-roll style, cut into ½-inch-thick pieces, and place them in the prepared muffin pans.

Bake for 20 to 25 minutes or until done.

Notes:

82 Cheese Rolls

2 cups all-purpose flour
5 tsp. baking powder
1 tsp. salt
2 T. shortening
¾ cup milk
1 cup grated cheese (Cheddar, Swiss, Monterey Jack, etc.)

Preheat the oven to 450°.

In a large bowl, whisk together the flour, baking powder, and salt. Cut in the shortening until the mixture resembles coarse crumbles. Gradually add the milk, and mix to form a soft dough. Turn out the dough onto a floured work surface and roll the dough thin to the shape of a rectangle; sprinkle on the cheese.

Beginning with one of the long sides, roll the dough into a log, like a jelly roll. Cut the log into 1-inch-thick pieces and place the cut side up on a greased baking sheet.

Bake for 12 minutes or until done.

Notes:

83 Cinnamon Fans

Fans
3 cups all-purpose flour
1 tsp. salt
4 tsp. baking powder
1 tsp. cream of tartar
⅓ cup sugar
¾ cup shortening
1 cup milk

Filling
½ cup (1 stick) butter, melted
    and cooled
½ cup sugar
2 T. cinnamon

Preheat the oven to 400°. Grease a 12-cup muffin pan and set aside.

For fans: Whisk together the flour, salt, baking powder, cream of tartar, and sugar. Cut in the shortening until the mixture resembles coarse crumbles. Add the milk and stir. Turn out onto a lightly floured surface and knead gently for a half minute.

Roll the dough about ¼ inch thick into a rectangle about 8 x 24 inches.

For filling: Spread the melted butter evenly on the dough. Mix together the sugar and cinnamon and then sprinkle the mixture evenly over the buttered dough.

Cut the dough into 4 long strips, each about 2 inches wide and 24 inches long. Stack the 4 strips on top of one another and then cut the stack into 12 equal pieces, each about 2 inches wide. Turn the pieces on their sides in greased muffin cups so each treat fans out.

Bake for 12 minutes or until golden brown.

Notes:

84 Cinnamon Rolls

Rolls
⅓ cup butter
1 12-ounce can evaporated milk
¾ cup sugar
3 T. active dry yeast
3 eggs
1 T. salt
4 cups all-purpose flour

Filling
¾ cup (1½ sticks) butter, softened
2 to 3 cups sugar
cinnamon
raisins and nuts (optional)

For rolls: In a small saucepan, heat the butter and evaporated milk until it reaches 115°.

In a large mixing bowl, mix together the evaporated milk mixture, sugar, and yeast. Let rest for 5 minutes. Add the eggs one at a time, mixing well after each addition. Add the salt and mix well. Slowly add the flour, mixing well as you add. Continue adding the flour until the dough begins to pull away from the sides of the bowl and forms a ball.

Turn out the dough onto a floured work surface and knead for 10 minutes, using as little flour as possible to keep the dough from sticking. Place the dough into a large greased bowl, turning the dough so the entire surface is greased. Cover and let rise until double, about 1 to 1½ hours.

ROLLS AND BUNS

Notes:

For filling: On a floured work surface, roll out the dough into a rectangle and spread with the butter, then the sugar. Sprinkle with cinnamon and then with the raisins and nuts (if desired). Starting at one of the long sides, roll dough into a log; cut into about 24 rolls. Place the rolls cut side up on 2 greased jelly roll pans, cover, and let rise again until double, about 45 minutes.

Preheat the oven to 350° and bake about 25 minutes or until done. These cinnamon rolls are great plain, but you can make a glaze by mixing together ½ cup powdered sugar and 2 to 3 teaspoons milk and spreading the glaze over the tops of the cinnamon rolls.

---

85 Cracked Wheat Potato Rolls

¾ cup cracked wheat	⅔ cup sugar
1 cup (2 sticks) butter	1 T. salt
3 cups boiling water	2 T. wheat germ (optional)
2 T. yeast	2 eggs
⅔ cup instant potato flakes	7 cups all-purpose flour, more
½ cup nonfat dry milk	or less

In a large bowl, combine cracked wheat, butter, and boiling water; cool to lukewarm. Add the remaining ingredients but only 2 cups of the flour. Beat with an electric mixer on medium speed for 3 minutes and then gradually add, by hand, enough of the remaining flour until the dough pulls away from the sides of the bowl.

Turn out the dough onto a floured work surface and knead for about 8 minutes. Place the dough into another large, greased bowl, turning the dough so the entire surface is greased. Cover and let rise until double, about 1½ hours.

Notes:

Punch down the dough and let it rest for about 5 minutes; shape into round rolls and place on greased baking sheets. Cover and let rise for 30 minutes.

Meanwhile, preheat the oven to 350°. Bake for 15 to 20 minutes or until done.

86 Dill Rolls

3 to 3½ cups all-purpose flour
¼ cup sugar
1 tsp. dill weed
1 tsp. salt
2¼ tsp. (1 package) active dry yeast
1½ cups milk
⅓ cup butter
1 egg

In a large bowl, whisk together 1½ cups of the flour with the sugar, dill weed, salt, and yeast.

In a small saucepan, heat the milk and butter until warm (120° to 130°). Add the warm milk mixture and the egg to the flour mixture and blend until moistened; beat for 3 minutes on medium speed. Stir in additional flour to make a stiff batter. Cover the bowl with a towel and let the batter rise until double, about 45 to 60 minutes.

Grease 18 muffin cups. Stir down the batter and then spoon it into the prepared muffin cups about ⅔ full. Cover with a towel and let rise until double, about 35 to 45 minutes.

Bake in a preheated 400° oven for 15 to 20 minutes or until done. Remove from the pans to cool on a wire rack.

Notes:

87 Easy Cinnamon Rolls

Cinnamon Rolls

¾ cup milk
¾ cup water
4½ tsp. (2 packages) active dry yeast
½ cup warm water (about 110°)
½ cup shortening
½ cup sugar

2 eggs
2 tsp. salt
7 cups all-purpose flour, more or less
½ cup (1 stick) butter, melted
cinnamon and sugar mixture

Glaze

1½ cups powdered sugar
2 to 3 T. water or milk

For rolls: In a saucepan, scald the milk and ¾ cup water. Pour the milk mixture into a large bowl and cool to lukewarm.

In a small bowl, dissolve the yeast in ½ cup warm water (110°) and let sit for 5 minutes.

In a large bowl, mix together the shortening, sugar, eggs, and salt. Add the milk mixture and stir well. Add the yeast mixture and stir well again. Add enough flour so the dough pulls away from the sides of the bowl. Turn out the dough onto a floured work surface and knead for about 5 minutes, adding more flour as needed to keep the dough from sticking.

Place the dough in a large greased bowl, turning the dough so the entire surface is greased. Cover and let rise until double, about 1 hour.

Turn out the dough onto a floured surface and roll it out to ¼-inch thickness. Cut with a biscuit cutter; then roll each piece out so it's long, narrow, and thin. Dip in melted butter and then dredge in the

Notes:

cinnamon and sugar mixture. Roll each piece up and place on greased baking sheets with their sides not quite touching. Cover and let rise about 40 to 45 minutes.

Preheated the oven to 350° and bake for 15 minutes or until done.

For glaze: Mix together the powdered sugar and water or milk and blend until smooth. Drizzle over cooled cinnamon rolls.

- -

88 German Sweet Rolls

4½ cups all-purpose flour,
    divided
1 tsp. salt
1 cup sugar
1 tsp. baking soda
2 tsp. cream of tartar

½ cup shortening
½ cup (1 stick) butter
2 eggs
¼ cup milk
¼ cup water
1 cup brown sugar

Preheat the oven to 375°.

In a large mixing bowl, whisk together 4 cups of the flour, salt, sugar, baking soda, and cream of tartar. Cut in the shortening and butter until the mixture resembles coarse crumbles. Beat one of the eggs and add it, along with the milk and water, to the flour mixture to form a soft dough.

In another bowl, beat the other egg; then add the brown sugar, and ½ cup flour, mixing well.

Roll the dough into a rectangle shape to ½-inch thickness and spread with the brown sugar mixture. Beginning with one of the long ends, roll up the dough like a jelly roll and cut into inch-thick slices. Place the rolls cut side up, about 2 inches apart, on greased baking sheets. Bake for 8 to 10 minutes or until done.

Notes:

89 Hamburger or Hot Dog Buns

2 T. active dry yeast
1 cup plus 2 T. warm water (about 110°)
⅓ cup cooking oil
¼ cup sugar
1 egg
1 tsp. salt
3 to 3½ cups all-purpose flour

In a large bowl, dissolve the yeast in the warm water. Add the cooking oil and sugar and mix again; let it sit until the yeast begins to bubble, about 10 minutes.

Add the egg, salt, and enough flour to form a soft dough. Turn out onto a floured surface and knead about 5 minutes. Do not let the dough rise.

Divide the dough into 12 pieces and shape each into a ball for a hamburger bun or a log for a hot dog bun. Place them 3 inches apart on greased cookie sheets. Cover and let rest for 15 minutes. Meanwhile, preheat the oven to 425°.

Bake for 8 to 12 minutes or until done and the tops are golden brown. Cool on wire racks and then slice them in half lengthwise to serve.

Notes:

90 Hoagie Rolls

2¼ tsp. (1 package) active dry yeast
2 T. sugar, divided
3 cups warm water, divided
¼ cup cooking oil
1 T. salt
8 to 8½ cups all-purpose flour

In a large bowl, dissolve the yeast and 1 tablespoon of sugar in ½ cup warm water (about 110°). Let stand until bubbly, about 5 to 10 minutes. Add the remaining water and sugar, and then mix in the oil, salt, and 4 cups of the flour. Using an electric mixer, beat on medium speed (or by hand using a large wooden spoon) for 3 minutes. Stir in enough of the remaining flour to form a soft dough.

Turn out the dough onto a floured work surface and knead for about 8 minutes, adding very small amounts of flour as needed to prevent sticking. Place the ball of kneaded dough into a greased bowl, turning the dough so the entire surface is greased. Cover and let rise until double, about 1 hour.

Punch down the dough and turn out onto a lightly floured surface. Divide the dough into 18 equal pieces. Shape each piece of dough into an oval and place them 2 inches apart on greased baking sheets. With a very sharp knife or kitchen scissors, slash the top of each piece ¼ inch deep. Cover the rolls with a towel and let rise again for 20 minutes. Meanwhile, preheat the oven to 400°.

Bake the rolls for 13 to 18 minutes or until they are a light golden color and done. Cool on wire racks before cutting open.

ROLLS AND BUNS

Notes:

91 Maple Buns

Buns
4½ tsp. (2 packages) active dry yeast
1¼ cups warm milk (about 110°)
3½ to 4 cups all-purpose flour
½ cup rolled oats
¼ cup sugar
¼ cup brown sugar
½ tsp. salt

¼ cup cooking oil

Filling
2 T. (¼ stick) butter, softened
¼ cup brown sugar
½ tsp. maple flavoring

Glaze
½ cup powdered sugar
⅛ tsp. maple flavoring
2 to 3 tsp. milk

For buns: In a small bowl, dissolve the yeast in the warm milk; let it sit until the mixture is a bit bubbly.

In a large bowl, whisk 1 cup of the flour with the rolled oats, sugar, brown sugar, and salt until well blended. Add the yeast mixture and the cooking oil to the flour mixture. Mix until well blended and then beat on medium speed for 3 minutes. Gradually stir in most of the remaining flour, just enough so the dough pulls away from the sides of the bowl.

Turn out the dough onto a floured surface and knead for about 10 minutes, adding flour as needed to prevent sticking. Cover the dough (use plastic wrap or a large bowl turned upside down) and let it rest for 25 minutes.

For filling: Roll the dough to a 12 x 16-inch rectangle. Spread the dough with the softened butter. Mix together the brown sugar and maple flavoring, and then sprinkle the mixture over the buttered dough. Starting with a 12-inch side, roll the dough into a tight log.

Notes:

Cut the log into 12 1-inch pieces. Place them in a greased 13 x 9-inch baking pan or jelly roll pan. Cover and let rise until double, about an hour.

Preheat the oven to 350° and bake for 20 to 30 minutes or until done. Cool 1 to 2 minutes and then remove the buns from the pan. Immediately make the glaze.

For glaze: Mix together all the glaze ingredients and then drizzle over the warm buns.

---

92 Mashed Potato Rolls

2¼ tsp. (1 package) active dry
    yeast
¼ cup warm water (about 110°)
1¾ cups warm milk (about
    110°)
¼ cup (½ stick) butter,
    softened to room
    temperature
¼ cup cooking oil

¾ cup sugar
1 egg
½ cup prepared mashed
    potatoes (see note below)
1½ tsp. salt
1 tsp. baking powder
½ tsp. baking soda
6 cups all-purpose flour
melted butter (optional)

In a large bowl, dissolve the yeast in warm water. Add the milk, butter, cooking oil, sugar, egg, and mashed potatoes and mix well. Stir in the salt, baking powder, baking soda, and half of the flour. Mix either by hand using a large wooden spoon or with an electric mixer, gradually adding flour until a soft dough is formed.

Turn out the dough onto a floured surface and knead for about 8 minutes. Place the dough in a large greased bowl, turning the dough so the entire surface is greased. Cover and let rise until double, about 1½ hours.

Notes:

Punch down the dough. Turn out onto a lightly floured surface and shape small amounts of dough into approximately 32 round balls. Place the balls 2 inches apart on greased baking sheets. Cover and let rise until double, about 30 to 45 minutes.

Bake in a preheated 375° oven for 15 to 18 minutes or until done and the tops are golden. Remove from the oven and, if desired, immediately brush the tops with melted butter. Set on wire racks to cool.

Note: If you don't have any leftover mashed potatoes and you're in a hurry, you can use dehydrated mashed potatoes. Just mix according to the package directions and use in place of fresh mashed potatoes.

93 Oatmeal Rolls

¾ cup warm water (about 110°)
4½ tsp. (2 packages) active dry yeast
½ cup brown sugar
3 tsp. salt
2 cups rolled oats (you can use quick-cooking or old-fashioned)
½ cup shortening
2 cups milk
2 eggs, beaten
6 cups all-purpose flour, more or less

In a small bowl, add the warm water and then sprinkle the yeast on top. Let stand for about 10 minutes.

In a large bowl, mix together the brown sugar, salt, and rolled oats. Cut in the shortening, using two forks, until the shortening is broken up.

Notes:

Scald the milk and pour it into the oat mixture; cool to lukewarm.

Add the beaten eggs, yeast mixture, and 1 cup of the flour; beat until well mixed. Let stand about 15 minutes until the batter is bubbly.

By hand, work in about 5 more cups of flour. Turn out the dough onto a floured work surface and knead for 5 minutes.

Place the dough in a large greased bowl, turning the dough so the entire surface is greased. Cover and let rise until double, about 1 to 1½ hours.

Shape the dough into balls, place onto greased baking sheets, cover, and let rise again until double, about 45 to 60 minutes.

Preheat the oven to 400° and bake for 10 to 15 minutes or until done.

- -

94 One-Week Make-Ahead Dinner Rolls

2¼ tsp. (1 package) active dry yeast
2 T. warm water (about 110°)
1 cup very hot water
1 tsp. salt
¾ cup shortening
¼ cup sugar
1 egg, well beaten
3½ cups all-purpose flour

In a small bowl, combine the yeast with warm water and set aside until bubbly, about 10 minutes.

Notes:

In a large mixing bowl, combine the hot water, salt, shortening, and sugar and mix well. Cool to lukewarm.

Add the yeast mixture to the hot water mixture, stir, and then add the beaten egg and half of the flour. Beat well for 3 minutes.

With a wooden spoon, stir in more of the flour, enough to make the dough easy to handle. (It will be softer than regular kneaded dough); cover and store in the refrigerator for up to a week.

When you want to bake some dinner rolls, take out the amount of dough needed. Shape into balls, slightly larger than golf-ball size, and put them in a greased baking pan or in greased muffin cups. Cover and let rise in a warm place until the dough warms up and doubles in bulk, about 2 to 2½ hours.

Preheat the oven to 425° and bake for 12 to 15 minutes or until done.

Notes:

95 Overnight Refrigerator Butter Crescent Rolls

2¼ tsp. (1 package) active dry yeast
2 T. warm water
¼ cup sugar
2 cups warm milk
1 egg, beaten
2 tsp. salt
5 to 6 cups all-purpose flour
½ cup (1 stick) butter, melted

In a large bowl, mix together the yeast, warm water, and sugar. When the yeast and sugar have dissolved, add the warm milk, egg, salt, and 2 cups of the flour. Mix well, add the melted butter, and mix again. Next, add enough of the remaining flour to make a smooth dough. (It won't be quite as firm as you would need for a kneaded dough.) Do not knead. Instead, cover the bowl and let it sit in your refrigerator overnight so the dough has a chance to stiffen up enough to handle the next day.

Several hours before you need the rolls, remove the bowl from the refrigerator, divide the dough into thirds, and then turn out the dough onto a floured work surface. Roll each piece of dough into a thin round. Cut each piece into 12 pie-shaped wedges. Roll up each wedge, from the outside to the center, into a crescent. Place them on a greased pan; don't crowd. Cover the pans and let the rolls rise until double, about 2 hours. (This could take a bit longer if the dough is very cold.)

Bake in a preheated 425° oven or until baked through and very lightly browned.

ROLLS AND BUNS

Notes:

96 Quick Caramel Rolls

Topping
½ cup brown sugar
½ cup (1 stick) butter, softened
2 T. light corn syrup

Filling
2 T. (¼ stick) butter, softened
¼ cup sugar
1 tsp. cinnamon

Rolls
3 to 3½ cups all-purpose flour
¼ cup sugar
1 tsp. salt
2¼ tsp. (1 package) active dry yeast
1 cup water
2 T. (¼ stick) butter
1 egg, beaten

For topping: Grease a 9 x 13-inch baking pan or jelly roll pan. In a small bowl, mix together the topping ingredients, blending well. Drop by spoonfuls onto the prepared pan and spread evenly. Set aside.

For rolls: In a large bowl, whisk 1½ cups of the flour with the sugar, salt, and yeast.

In a small saucepan, heat the water and butter to about 125°. Pour into the flour mixture, add the beaten egg, and beat the mixture for 3 minutes. Gradually stir in most of the remaining flour until the dough pulls away from the sides of the bowl.

Turn out the dough onto a floured surface and knead for 1 minute. Roll out the dough to a 15 x 7-inch rectangle. Set aside while you make the filling.

For filling: Evenly spread the butter over the dough. Mix the sugar and cinnamon together and sprinkle evenly over the buttered dough.

Notes:

Starting with a 15-inch side, roll the dough into a tight log. Cut into 12 rounds and place cut side down in the prepared baking pan. Cover and let rise until double, about 45 minutes.

Preheat the oven to 375° and bake for 25 to 30 minutes or until done. Allow the rolls to cool in the pan for one minute before turning them out onto a serving platter.

---

97 Rye Rolls

1 to 1¼ cups all-purpose flour	1 cup milk
2 T. sugar	2 T. shortening
1 tsp. caraway seeds	1 egg
1 tsp. salt	1 cup rye flour
2¼ tsp. (1 package) active dry yeast	melted butter for brushing tops of rolls

In a large bowl, whisk ¾ cup all-purpose flour with the sugar, caraway seeds, salt, and yeast.

In a small saucepan, heat the milk and shortening to 120° to 130°. Add the warm milk mixture and the egg to the flour mixture and blend; beat for 3 minutes on medium speed. Add the rye flour and beat well; then add enough of the remaining all-purpose flour to make a stiff batter.

Grease a muffin pan; spoon the batter into the prepared muffin cups to ⅔ full and let the batter rise, uncovered, for about 25 to 30 minutes in a warm place. In the meantime, preheat the oven to 400°.

Bake the rolls for 12 to 15 minutes or until done. Brush tops with melted butter.

Notes:

98 Sticky Buns

¼ tsp. baking soda
¼ cup sugar
1 tsp. salt
2¼ tsp. (1 package) active dry yeast
3 cups all-purpose flour
1 cup buttermilk
3 T. cooking oil
¼ cup water
¾ cup (¾ stick) butter, melted and cooled
¾ cup brown sugar
¾ cup pecans, broken or chopped
1 tsp. cinnamon

In a large bowl, whisk together the baking soda, sugar, salt, yeast, and 1 cup of the flour.

In a saucepan, heat the buttermilk and cooking oil over medium heat until warm (about 120°); add the buttermilk mixture to the flour mixture and beat on high speed for 2 minutes. Stir in 1½ cups of the remaining flour and beat with a wooden spoon until smooth.

Using a portion of the remaining flour, lightly flour a clean surface and turn out the dough. Knead for about 8 minutes, adding more flour as needed to prevent sticking. Let the dough rest on the work surface while preparing the muffin pans.

In a small bowl, combine the water, 4 tablespoons of the melted butter, and ½ cup of the brown sugar. Distribute the mixture evenly among 12 muffin cups. Top with the pecans, evenly divided between the muffin cups.

Notes:

Roll out the dough into a 12 x 15-inch rectangle. Brush the dough with the remaining 2 tablespoons of melted butter. Combine the cinnamon with the remaining ¼ cup brown sugar and sprinkle evenly over the buttered dough.

Starting at a shorter end, roll up the dough into a log. (It will be about 12 inches long.) Cut into 12 equal rounds and place them, cut side down, in the prepared muffin cups. Let rise until doubled (about 1 to 1½ hours).

Preheat the oven to 350° and bake for 25 minutes or until done. Remove the pans from the oven and immediately invert onto serving plates, leaving the pans inverted over the rolls so the melted syrup and pecans have a chance to drip from the pan onto the rolls. Remove the pans and allow the sticky buns to cool for another 10 minutes before eating.

99 Sweet Cream Buns

Buns
1½ cups milk
¼ cup plus 1 T. sugar, divided
2¼ tsp. salt
¾ cup shortening
¾ cup warm water (about 115°)
3 T. (or use 3 packages) active dry yeast
3 eggs, beaten
7 cups all-purpose flour, more or less

Notes:

Filling
¼ cup shortening
½ cup milk
1 tsp. vanilla
3 cups powdered sugar

For buns: Scald the milk; then pour into a large bowl and add ¼ cup sugar, salt, and shortening. Stir to dissolve and then cool to lukewarm.

In a small bowl, add warm water and 1 tablespoon sugar; stir until dissolved. Sprinkle the yeast on top and let it stand for 10 minutes.

Beat the sugar and water mixture with a fork and then pour it into the milk mixture, stirring to mix. Add the beaten eggs and mix again.

Stir in 4 cups of the flour and beat on medium speed for 3 minutes. By hand, work in just enough flour (about 3 more cups) to form a soft dough that pulls away from the sides of the bowl. Turn the dough out onto a floured work surface and knead for 5 to 6 minutes.

Place the dough in a greased bowl, turning the dough so the entire surface is greased. Cover and let rise until double, about 1½ hours.

Punch down the dough, separate it into 48 equal pieces, and shape the pieces into balls. Place them in greased baking pans (jelly roll pans work well); cover and let rise until double, about 1 hour.

Bake in a preheated 375° oven for 25 minutes or until done.

For filling: Using an electric mixer on low speed, beat together the shortening, milk, and vanilla. Gradually add the powdered sugar, beating well after each addition; continue beating until the filling is light and fluffy. Just before serving, cut a slit in each bun and fill with the filling.

Notes:

120

RECIPE INDEX

Muffins

RECIPE INDEX

Notes:

Rolls and Buns

RECIPE INDEX

Notes:

99 Favorite Amish Recipes
Bring the Simple Life Home

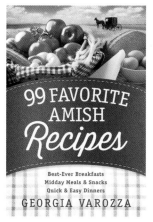

The Amish are admired for their simple life, their intricate quilts, their forthright faith, and their homemade meals. Straight from the heart of Amish country, this new collection of hearty, wholesome recipes will remind you of the pleasures of the family table.

Learn to prepare easy and delicious dishes for your loved ones, including

- caramel apple pie
- farmer's stew
- shoo-fly pie
- haystack supper
- homemade noodles

Find new favorites, make new traditions, and discover the pleasure of old-fashioned food!

501 Time-Saving Tips Every Woman Should Know

Get More Done in Less Time with Less Stress

Would you like some help with your to-do list? Who wouldn't! You'll love these surprisingly quick, easy, and effective ways to complete troublesome tasks in a snap.

- A squeegee or dryer sheet works great for removing pet hair from your furniture and carpet.
- Plain, whole-milk yogurt and a cold-water rinse soothe sunburned skin.
- Add Epsom salts to your watering can to make your garden more productive.
- Put baking soda and vinegar to work removing spots from your old baking pans.
- Use ice cubes to restore your carpet where furniture has left indentations.

You don't have to work harder. Just get smarter—and enjoy the time you'll save.

The Homestyle Amish Kitchen Cookbook

Let a Little Plain Cooking Warm Up Your Life

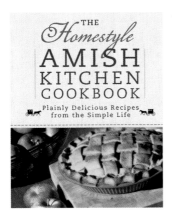

Who doesn't want simplicity in the kitchen?

Most of these delicious, easy-to-make dishes are simplicity itself. The Amish are a productive and busy people. They work hard in the home and on their farms, and they need good, filling food that doesn't require a lot of preparation and time. A few basic ingredients, some savory and sweet spices, and a little love make many of these meals a cook's delight. And if you want something a bit more complex and impressive, those recipes are here for you too.

Along with fascinating tidbits about the Amish way of life, you will find directions for lovely, old-fashioned food such as

- scrapple
- honey oatmeal bread
- coffee beef stew
- potato rivvel soup
- snitz and knepp
- shoo-fly pie

Everything from breakfast to dessert is covered in this celebration of comfort food and family. Hundreds of irresistible options will help you bring the simple life to your own home and kitchen.

The Amish Canning Cookbook

Full Pantry, Full Heart

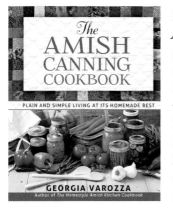

From the author of *The Homestyle Amish Kitchen Cookbook* comes a great new collection of recipes, hints, and Plain wisdom for everyone who loves the idea of preserving fresh, wholesome food. Whether you're a beginning canner or a seasoned cook honing her skills, certified Master Food Preserver Georgia Varozza will show you how to get the very best out of your food. You'll find...

- a short history of canning
- lists of all the tools and supplies you need to get started
- basic instructions for safe canning
- recipes for canning fruit, vegetables, meat, soups, sauces, and more
- guidelines for safely adapting recipes to fit your family's tastes

With its expert advice and warm tones, *The Amish Canning Cookbook* will become a beloved companion to everyone who loves the tradition, frugality, and homestyle flavor of Amish cooking!

To learn more about Harvest House books and
to read sample chapters, visit our website:

www.harvesthousepublishers.com

HARVEST HOUSE PUBLISHERS
EUGENE, OREGON